"This book addresses many of the complaints and issues that I hear every day when I talk to teens and parents in the office. The stories are familiar, and the solutions are logical, effective, and practical. I recommend it enthusiastically to any teen who wants to improve their sleep habits."

—**Nelson Branco, MD, FAAP**, pediatrician with over twenty years' experience who practices at Tamalpais Pediatrics in Marin County, CA; and associate clinical professor in the department of pediatrics at the University of California, San Francisco

"Finally, an evidence-based, easy-to-read, and sure-to-work guide for teens with sleep problems. What took so long! I will be using this *sleep science* workbook with all the teens who come to me seeking solutions to the age-old problem of insomnia. Tompkins and Thompson are incredibly thorough, addressing the many micro parts that in combination will help set up teens for healthy sleep and wellness. They have designed playful yet informative assessments for teens to better understand their personalized needs, as well as to examine the impact of their values, attitudes, thoughts, and actions on sleep. Not only do the authors present effective ideas and plans to implement at night, but do so for the daytime as well, since as they the experts know, how well we sleep has a lot to do with how we spend our days. This workbook is a much-needed addition to our youth literature, supporting youth in one of their most important daily tasks—getting their Zzzs!"

—**Katherine Martinez, PsyD, RPsych**, psychologist in practice at the Vancouver CBT Centre in Vancouver, BC, Canada, and coauthor of *Your Anxious Mind*

"Tompkins and Thompson have produced a concise, well-organized, and useful tool that should be on the bookshelf—or better yet in the hands—of any clinician working with teens. Asking about sleep and providing useful interventions to promote adequate sleep are among the most useful interventions clinicians can make for a large majority of teens in the US. For teens who recognize the problem and want to solve it, this workbook offers straight talk and practical solutions."

—**Glen R. Elliot, PhD, MD**, chief psychiatrist and medical director at the Children's Health Council; clinical professor emeritus of child and adolescent psychiatry at the University of California, San Francisco; clinical professor (Affiliated) of child and adolescent psychiatry at Stanford School of Medicine

"Sleep problems are among the most common complaints that plague adolescents in their passage through high school. Although they will admit to sleep issues, they seem unwilling to accept guidance regarding remedies. *The Insomnia Workbook for Teens* will provide an invaluable resource for both health care professionals and parents. If the individual has the motivation to want to improve the problem, the workbook provides the means for the teen to fix themselves. In a very logical and readable approach, Tompkins and Thompson guide the sleep-deprived adolescent though exercises, sprinkled with case histories, that will allow the teen to achieve a self-paced solution."

> —**Richard L. Oken, MD, FAAP,** pediatrician for over forty years at East Bay Pediatric Medical Group, and clinical professor in the department of pediatrics at the University of California, San Francisco

"Sleep problems in young patients are on the rise and contribute to many other emotional as well as behavioral difficulties. Good self-help tools are desperately needed by patients and clinicians alike. Tompkins and Thompson masterfully fill this need with this outstanding, valuable resource. Written in a clear, developmentally accessible, and engaging manner, the workbook offers pertinent information and actionable exercises for improving sleep practices. I enthusiastically recommend the workbook and encourage its widespread use!"

> —**Robert D. Friedberg, PhD, ABPP,** professor, head of child emphasis area, Palo Alto University

"Tompkins and Thompson have crafted a step-by-step masterpiece to support teens in battling insomnia and achieving healthy sleep patterns. The activities included are evidence-based, grounded in theory, and demonstrated effective. This book is a must-have for parents and teens who are struggling with insomnia, as well as clinicians working with this population."

> —**Eric Storch, PhD,** McIngvale Presidential Endowed Chair and Professor, Menninger Department of Psychiatry and Behavioral Sciences, Baylor College of Medicine

"Rarely has there been a guide so clear, concise, and practical for adolescents as *The Insomnia Workbook for Teens*. Tompkins and Thompson cut through the hyperbole of arguments and blame with a teenager to guide all readers towards a realistic, straightforward path through this all-too-common nocturnal obstacle to healthy rest and sleep. Informative and realistic, *The Insomnia Workbook for Teens* should be on the desk of every pediatrician, therapist, and parent!"

> —**Brad D. Berman, MD, FAAP**, practitioner of developmental-behavioral pediatrics in the San Francisco Bay Area for thirty years at Progressions: Developmental Pediatrics; clinical professor of pediatrics at UCSF Benioff Children's Hospital

"The importance of sleep to one's well-being cannot be overstated. Unfortunately, its importance is too often overlooked or not sufficiently prioritized. Effective nonmedication treatment for insomnia is available, and fortunately, in *The Insomnia Workbook for Teens*, Tompkins and Thompson make it highly accessible to teenagers. The practical skills they offer can be useful to teens working through their insomnia on their own and as an adjunct to professional assistance when that is required. I enthusiastically recommend this workbook to teens struggling with insomnia as well as their parents and health care professionals!"

> —**R. Trent Codd, III, EdS, LPC, BCBA**, executive director of the Cognitive-Behavioral Therapy Center of Western North Carolina, and coauthor of *Teaching and Supervising Cognitive Behavioral Therapy* and *Practice-Based Research*

"Adolescent sleep problems are an epidemic concern with serious mental, physical, and educational consequences. *The Insomnia Workbook for Teens* is a much-needed and extremely valuable resource to help youth learn healthy sleep habits and effective strategies to manage the stress and anxiety that typically underlie sleep problems. Written by two leading mental health experts, the workbook provides a highly structured and easy-to-follow program that guides teens through a series of steps to identify and correct the full range of factors, including diet and excessive screen time, contributing to poor sleep. This workbook is a must for teens, therapists, and parents."

> —**John Piacentini, PhD, ABPP**, professor and director; Center for Child Anxiety, Resilience, Education and Support; UCLA Semel Institute for Neuroscience and Human Behavior

"Psychology and neuroscience have established numerous ways in which sleep contributes to creating and maintaining a healthy body, brain, and mind. To a large degree, education and interventions related to sleep have not kept pace with the important discoveries of the science. This marvelous book provides easy-to-use tools to assist teens in developing and maintaining healthy sleep. And the tools work for adults as well. Better sleep makes everything better."

—**David E. Presti**, clinical psychologist; professor in the department of neurobiology at the University of California, Berkeley; and author of *Foundational Concepts in Neuroscience*

*"The Insomnia Workbook for Teens* is essential reading for all teens who struggle with getting enough sleep and who want a nonjudgmental guide to help them understand more about themselves. I love the way the authors guide and educate the reader in learning strategies that are unique to their style, whether they are a night owl or a morning lark. Parents, teachers, and mental health professionals will benefit as well, as they discover new ways to approach the prevalent stress and worry the teens they care for experience on a daily basis."

—**Rona Renner, RN**, parenting coach and author of *Is That Me Yelling?*

*"The Insomnia Workbook for Teens* is filled with practical advice and activities. It will benefit many teens with just about any type of sleep difficulty. Rather than putting them to sleep, this workbook will help them learn about good sleep and give them the tools they need to sleep better.… All in all, this is a great resource for anyone who wishes to help teens sleep better. I highly recommend it!"

—**Ann M. Kring, PhD**, professor and chair in the department of psychology at the University of California, Berkeley

# the insomnia workbook for teens

## skills to help you stop stressing & start sleeping better

MICHAEL A. TOMPKINS, PhD
MONIQUE A. THOMPSON, PsyD

Instant Help Books
An Imprint of New Harbinger Publications, Inc.

## Publisher's Note

*This publication is designed to provide accurate and authoritative information in regard to the subject matter covered. It is sold with the understanding that the publisher is not engaged in rendering psychological, financial, legal, or other professional services. If expert assistance or counseling is needed, the services of a competent professional should be sought.*

Distributed in Canada by Raincoast Books

Copyright © 2018 by Michael A. Tompkins and Monique A. Thompson
New Harbinger Publications, Inc.
5674 Shattuck Avenue
Oakland, CA 94609
www.newharbinger.com

Cover design by Amy Shoup

Acquired by Tesilya Hanauer

Edited by Will DeRooy

Library of Congress Cataloging-in-Publication Data on file

20    19    18

10    9    8    7    6    5    4    3    2    1          First Printing (REVISED)

For the morning larks and night owls in our homes.

# contents

Does it seem like it takes hours for you to fall asleep? Or do you wake up in the middle of the night and can't fall back to sleep? Well, you've got company. About 40 percent of teens report some insomnia symptoms. The good news is that there's something—in fact a lot of things—you can do about it. And you've come to the right place to figure it out.

This workbook is scientifically sound. And it's practical. It will teach you how to diagnose your problems. And it will teach you skills. The beautiful part about it is that you'll be able to use these skills for your whole life. It's great that you're going to work on your sleep problem now. Sometimes people wait years and years and years to get help.

There are so many advantages to sleeping better. Some are obvious—you'll have more energy, you'll be more alert, you'll be less irritable. But there are other benefits, too. You are likely to feel less stressed and more positive. You're likely to be more motivated to do what you have to do. You'll be able to pay attention better. You'll be more coordinated and less likely to get hurt. Your health will be better. You'll even look better. Everything is easier when you're sleeping well. And everything is harder when you're not.

Here's good news. There's a psychological treatment for sleep problems that is called cognitive behavioral therapy for insomnia (CBT-I) and it works great—even better than sleep medications—and we have the science to prove it. CBT-I is effective and brief, and the benefits are long lasting. The skills take practice, but anybody can learn them.

The activities in this workbook are easy to learn. Each activity rests on solid sleep science. They contain cognitive techniques to help you change your unhelpful thinking, along with techniques to help you change your unhelpful behaviors. You're going to learn about insomnia, some basic sleep science, and setting realistic sleep goals. One really important part is the Good Sleep Attitude. Insomnia is all about trying too hard. You're trying to get to sleep—but sleep doesn't work that way. In fact, the harder you try to make yourself sleep, the more you actually push sleep away. You'll also learn what to do before you get in bed, while you're trying to fall asleep or fall back to sleep, when you wake up in the morning, and during the day. And, you'll learn how to manage your sleep worries.

The authors wrote this book specifically for you, the teenager who is desperate to sleep but can't. If you have suffered with insomnia for months or even years, you may believe that you'll never sleep well again. But follow the instructions in this workbook. Take one step at a time, and you'll soon be sleeping better and longer. You'll be back to sleeping the good sleep.

—Judith S. Beck, PhD
President, Beck Institute for Cognitive Behavior Therapy
Clinical professor of psychology in psychiatry, University of Pennsylvania

Sleep is food for the brain, particularly for the developing brains of teens. Yet you're probably not getting enough of it. More than half of people aged fifteen to nineteen are getting less than six hours of sleep and therefore are two hours short of the eight-hour minimum recommendation. A brain that is hungry for sleep will get it, even when you don't expect it. You might fall asleep in the middle of your studies or while doing something important, with drastic consequences. Excessive sleepiness is a big cause of accidents in the United States. Drowsiness behind the wheel leads to more than 100,000 auto crashes every year. In addition, sleep-deprived teens don't do as well in school or on the athletic field and may feel more anxious, stressed, and moody. Also, sleep-deprived teens look haggard and sickly and aren't as attractive to other teens as those who are well-rested. Can you believe it?

There are likely many reasons that you're not getting enough sleep. Some of those reasons are things you can't do much about, such as changes in your developing brain. Now that you're a teenager, your brain wants to put off sleep more than when you were a child, making it hard for you to fall asleep before 11:00 p.m. and wake up for school on time. In addition, social media, electronic devices, late-night homework, and an irregular sleep pattern (staying up late during the week and sleeping in on weekends) may contribute to trouble getting adequate sleep. However, there are things that you *can* do something about, and the skills taught in this workbook will help. In fact, your mind and body know how to sleep. Sleep is hardwired—it's a natural process in humans, just as it is in other animals. If you're having trouble sleeping, it's likely that you've gotten in the way of this natural process. The activities in this workbook will help you get out of the way of your brain's desire to sleep, so that you'll start to sleep well again.

Most of the activities are organized around different periods in the night and day (for example, Before Bed, In Bed and Waiting for Sleep to Come, Out of Bed in the Morning, and Out of Bed During the Day). You'll learn specific things you can do in each of these periods that can improve your sleep. Most of the activities will be easy for you to learn and practice, but some may be difficult, such as changing your sleep habits. Yet changing your sleep habits is probably one of the best things you can do to improve your sleep.

You may benefit from the support of a mental health counselor as you learn and practice the activities, since this book is not meant to take the place of counseling. A counselor can also help you select the activities that are the best fit for you and for your particular sleep problems. Furthermore, we recommend that you speak to your physician about your sleep difficulties. It may be the case that a medical problem is affecting your ability to sleep, and, if so, your physician can help.

Last, we hope that once you do the activities and learn the skills, you'll use them over and over throughout your life to ensure you get a good night's rest.

If working with teens is a big part of your practice, you likely are aware that many, if not most, of the teens you see have some trouble sleeping. Sleep is the most sensitive measure of our emotional well-being, and if clients are anxious, depressed, or irritable, they likely are having problems with sleep too. Fortunately, there are now effective nonmedication treatments for insomnia and sleep difficulties. As a mental health professional, you play a key role in supporting teens as they learn and practice the powerful skills in this workbook, skills that will help them enjoy healthier and more restorative sleep.

Workbooks are not a substitute for thoughtful and creative therapists. Creative and flexible application of the activities in this workbook is the key to correcting your teen client's insomnia. We encourage you to select activities that target the teen's unique difficulties and your understanding of the teen's strengths and weaknesses. For example, although we have strived to make the activities as simple and easy to use as possible, you may wish to further simplify an activity if it seems too abstract for your client or shorten an activity if your client struggles with attention issues. Most teens will have the cognitive capacity to benefit from the activities presented. Nevertheless, you'll wish to adjust the activities to match your clients' developmental age to ensure that they will learn and benefit from each skill. We've created a supplemental clinician's guide with more guidance and suggestions for using the activities in this workbook with your teen clients. Find it at http://www.newharbinger.com/41245.

Last, although the activities in this book are appropriate for any teen who seeks help for insomnia, activities 28 to 31 should prove especially beneficial for those who may have an anxiety disorder. If further assistance with excessive worry, anxiety, and fear is called for, we encourage you to check the New Harbinger Publications website (www. newharbinger.com) for many excellent workbooks, such as the *Relaxation and Stress Reduction Workbook for Teens* and the *Anxiety Workbook for Teens*, for you to use with the activities in this workbook.

Particularly when teen clients have experienced significant and chronic sleep problems, we strongly recommend you refer teen clients to their physician to rule out the presence of sleep apnea, diabetes, thyroid disease, or any other medical condition that may result in poor sleep.

# 1 typical sleep stories

## for you to know

Although all teens sleep, teens who don't sleep well tend to have different sleep stories than those who do. Some teens have trouble falling asleep when they turn out the light. Other teens go to sleep quickly but awaken in the night and have a hard time falling back asleep. And every teen with insomnia tries in his or her own way to get to sleep and stay asleep, but often these strategies just contribute to the problem in some way. Sleep patterns differ from teen to teen, and over months or even years a "sleep story" begins to take shape. Knowing your unique sleep story will direct you to the activities in this book that, with practice, will help you get a good night's sleep again.

## for you to do

Read the sleep stories of these three teens, and then answer the questions that follow.

### ✱ Conrad

*Conrad is a busy sixteen-year-old. He plays basketball and is a member of several school clubs. He lives with his mother and his seven-year-old sister. He doesn't feel tired until late in the evening, and he struggles to get out of bed in the morning. He gets home late after basketball practice, and his mom and sister have often already eaten dinner because his sister's bedtime is eight thirty. He tends to work on his homework in his bedroom but isn't very productive. He's tired from the day and is often distracted by social media and online video games. He would like to fall asleep by midnight so he can wake up by seven, but he's usually up past two. He and his mom argue every night about going to sleep and* in the morning about getting out of bed. Every weekday morning, he goes to school tired and irritated with his mom. He's still doing well at school, but he often naps in class. He's thinking about quitting the basketball team because he's too tired and too stressed to fit basketball in with everything else he has to do.

## ✱ Charlotte

Charlotte is fourteen years old and is beginning to struggle at school because she's so tired that she's having trouble concentrating on her work. She doesn't have a lot of after-school activities, so she takes a two-hour nap when she gets home so that she has the energy to face her homework. She enjoys her time alone before her parents get home from work. She spends it surfing the Internet and chatting with friends on social media. Once her parents are home, they begin to nag her to get off her cell phone and start her homework. After a couple of hours, her parents start to nag her to finish her homework and go to bed. She tells them that she needs more time. They tell her that she needs to sleep. Sometimes she gets so frustrated with her parents and her homework that she cries. Once she's in bed, she has a hard time winding down. She thinks about the things that happened that day or worries about what might happen tomorrow. In the morning, she's tired and cranky.

## ✱ Keaton

Keaton doesn't have a hard time getting to bed on time. But after she turns off the lights, she can't relax and fall asleep. She reviews the day and makes a mental to-do list for the following day. After a while, she starts to worry about this and that—the argument she had with a friend, tomorrow's math test, the essay due in two weeks. She often lies in bed awake for an hour and a half, and once she does fall asleep, she awakens in an hour or two and starts to worry again, but this time she's worrying about not getting enough sleep. She awakens earlier than she needs to because she's already started to think about all the tasks ahead of her that'll be more difficult because she didn't sleep well. She has started to dread nighttime. She feels frustrated and powerless and is beginning to wonder whether things will ever change for her.

1. Which of these sleep stories is most like yours and why?

   _____

   _____

   _____

2. Maybe parts of all three stories rang a bell. Were there other themes or issues in any of the stories that sound a bit like your sleep story? What were they?

   _____

   _____

   _____

3. Like every story, your sleep story has a beginning, a middle, and an end—from morning to evening and to morning again. What's your sleep story? Is it like a Stephen King novel, where every night is a nightmare?

   _____

   _____

   _____

   _____

   _____

   _____

   _____

4. If you could rewrite your sleep story from a nightmare to a feel-good story, what would you change?

_____

_____

_____

_____

_____

# more to do

Often, at the heart of every sleep story is a sleep type. Sometimes, your sleep type isn't a great match with the sleep type of your mom or dad or your brothers or sisters.

1. Following are some common sleep types. Indicate how much each one reminds you of yourself or someone in your family.

| | | |
|---|---|---|
| **Night Owl** | Night owls find that they aren't tired until very late in the evening. While an 11:00 p.m. bedtime would give them enough sleep, they don't feel sleepy until hours later. | ☐ Totally<br>☐ Kind of<br>☐ Not at all |
| **Morning Lark** | Larks prefer to go to bed early in the evening and get up early the next day. They awaken easily in the morning and are ready to go, with lots of energy. | ☐ Totally<br>☐ Kind of<br>☐ Not at all |
| **Worry-wart** | Worrywarts worry that they won't fall asleep, that they aren't getting enough sleep, and that if they wake up in the night they won't fall back asleep. They also worry about a ton of other things. All this worry pushes sleep away. | ☐ Totally<br>☐ Kind of<br>☐ Not at all |
| **Put-It-Offer** | Put-it-offers intend to get their homework or other tasks done before bedtime but often find other things to do first. As bedtime approaches, they realize that they have more to do than they can get done by bedtime. They then pull an all-nighter—or stay up late to finish everything they put off doing earlier—and arrive at school or work exhausted and cranky. | ☐ Totally<br>☐ Kind of<br>☐ Not at all |

| Screen-somniac | Screen-somniacs *can* sleep but would rather stay up late watching shows and interacting with friends on social media. They then try to go to sleep immediately after they turn off their screens rather than "disconnecting" earlier in the evening. | ☐ Totally<br>☐ Kind of<br>☐ Not at all |
|---|---|---|

2. Which sleep type reminds you most of yourself? What is it about the particular sleep type that is most like you?

_____

_____

_____

3. How does your sleep type compare to your mom's or dad's sleep type, or your brother's or sister's sleep type? Is Mom a morning lark, whereas Dad is a night owl? What happens in your house when the people who share a roof don't have similar sleep types?

_____

_____

_____

# 2 the chapters of your sleep story

## for you to know

Your sleep story, like any story, has parts or chapters. Each chapter describes the things that you're usually thinking, feeling, and doing at a certain time of day:

Before Bed

In Bed and Waiting for Sleep to Come

In Bed and Waiting for Sleep to Come *Back*

Out of Bed in the Morning

During the Day at School

During the Day After School

How much you sleep or how well you sleep depends on more than what you do at night. It depends on the things that you do or don't do during the day too. By examining each chapter in your sleep story—what typically happens during the different periods of your day—you'll identify the problems that contribute to your sleep troubles. Once you know your full sleep story, you can apply the skills you'll learn in this book to rewrite your sleep story from one of poor sleep to one of good sleep.

# for you to do

Give the details of your sleep story. In the following worksheet, write down some of the typical thoughts you have about sleep, as well as what you're feeling and doing in general, at each time of day. In the "Before Bed" section are examples from teens we've worked with. Circle **Y** (yes) if the thought, feeling, or behavior is true for you or **N** (no) if it's not; then write in other thoughts, feelings, and behaviors of your own. Then fill in the remaining chapters of your sleep story.

| Before Bed | | |
|---|---|---|
| What I'm thinking: | *Yay, it's time for bed! I'm sleepy and ready to get some shut-eye!* | Y/N |
| | *Time for bed. It was a full day, and now it's time to get some rest.* | Y/N |
| | *Oh no, it's bedtime and I have so many things to do! I'm too keyed up to sleep!* | Y/N |
| | *I know that I won't fall asleep, so I might as well not even try.* | Y/N |
| | *Why is my mom making me go to bed?! I have other things that I need to do!* | Y/N |
| | Other: | |
| | Other: | |

| | | |
|---|---|---|
| What I'm feeling: | Relaxed | Y/N |
| | Happy | Y/N |
| | Worried | Y/N |
| | Sad | Y/N |
| | Angry | Y/N |
| | Other: | |
| | Other: | |
| What I'm doing: | Relaxing with my family or pets | Y/N |
| | Watching YouTube on my phone in my room | Y/N |
| | Thinking about negative things that happened during the day | Y/N |
| | Trying to finish my homework! | Y/N |
| | Arguing with my parents | Y/N |
| | Other: | |
| | Other: | |

| In Bed and Waiting for Sleep to Come | | |
|---|---|---|
| What I'm thinking: | | |
| | | |
| | | |
| | | |
| | | |
| What I'm feeling: | | |
| | | |
| | | |
| | | |
| | | |
| What I'm doing: | | |
| | | |
| | | |
| | | |
| | | |

| In Bed and Waiting for Sleep to Come Back | | |
|---|---|---|
| What I'm thinking: | | |
| | | |
| | | |
| | | |
| | | |
| What I'm feeling: | | |
| | | |
| | | |
| | | |
| | | |
| What I'm doing: | | |
| | | |
| | | |
| | | |
| | | |

| Out of Bed in the Morning | | |
|---|---|---|
| What I'm thinking: | | |
| | | |
| | | |
| | | |
| | | |
| What I'm feeling: | | |
| | | |
| | | |
| | | |
| | | |
| What I'm doing: | | |
| | | |
| | | |
| | | |
| | | |

| During the Day at School | | |
|---|---|---|
| What I'm thinking: | | |
| What I'm feeling: | | |
| What I'm doing: | | |

| During the Day After School | | |
|---|---|---|
| What I'm thinking: | | |
| | | |
| | | |
| | | |
| | | |
| What I'm feeling: | | |
| | | |
| | | |
| | | |
| | | |
| What I'm doing: | | |
| | | |
| | | |
| | | |
| | | |

# more to do

It's official! You're a typical teen with your own unique sleep story. Knowing your full sleep story, and every chapter in it, is the first step toward sleeping well.

1. Look at the thoughts, feelings, and doings you circled **Y** in response to (or what you wrote in the blanks) for the "Before Bed" chapter of your sleep story. Mark with an **X** each one you think might be a *sleep hazard*: a thought, feeling, or behavior that prevents sleep from coming. Mark with an **O** each one you think might be a *sleep helper*: a thought, feeling, or behavior that encourages and enables sleep to come. Do the same in the other chapters of your sleep story—mark each potential sleep hazard with **X** and each sleep helper with **O**.

2. In the following chart, tally your hazards and helpers to identify which chapters of your sleep story are trouble zones. If the number of hazards is similar to the number of helpers, check "Maybe."

| Chapter | Number of Sleep Hazards (X) | Number of Sleep Helpers (O) | Trouble Zone? |
|---|---|---|---|
| Before Bed | | | ☐ Yes<br>☐ Maybe<br>☐ No |
| In Bed and Waiting for Sleep to Come | | | ☐ Yes<br>☐ Maybe<br>☐ No |
| In Bed and Waiting for Sleep to Come Back | | | ☐ Yes<br>☐ Maybe<br>☐ No |

| | | | |
|---|---|---|---|
| Out of Bed in the Morning | | | ☐ Yes<br>☐ Maybe<br>☐ No |
| During the Day at School | | | ☐ Yes<br>☐ Maybe<br>☐ No |
| During the Day After School | | | ☐ Yes<br>☐ Maybe<br>☐ No |

3. Now that you've identified the sleep chapters that contribute most to your poor sleep story, what do you think are the possible causes (and solutions)?

_____

_____

_____

# 3 sleep hazards and helpers across the day

## for you to know

As you've learned, every teen's sleep story is a little different, but all sleep stories—good sleep stories and bad sleep stories—share certain elements. These elements are the sleep hazards and sleep helpers that influence how quickly sleep comes and stays. These are the things that you think, feel, or do to *get* to sleep or to *stay* asleep. Knowing a sleep helper from a sleep hazard is essential if you want to develop a plan to get a good night's sleep.

## for you to do

In the following table are typical teen behaviors, grouped according to the six chapters of your sleep story. For each behavior, ask yourself (a) *Is this behavior (or one very much like it) part of my sleep story?* and (b) *Do I think it tends to* help *or* hinder *my sleep?* (You might want to refer to what you wrote down in the previous activity.)

| Behavior | How Often Do I Do This? | Sleep Hazard or Helper? |
|---|---|---|
| **Before Bed** | | |
| Realize that I have more homework than I thought and decide to stay up late to finish. | ☐ All the time  ☐ Sometimes  ☐ Never | ☐ Hazard  ☐ Helper |
| Check with my family about the next day's activities and plans. | ☐ All the time  ☐ Sometimes  ☐ Never | ☐ Hazard  ☐ Helper |

| Go off screens about an hour before I go to bed to relax and wind down. | ☐ All the time ☐ Sometimes ☐ Never | ☐ Hazard ☐ Helper |
|---|---|---|
| Watch television or do homework on my computer in bed until it's time to turn off the lights. | ☐ All the time ☐ Sometimes ☐ Never | ☐ Hazard ☐ Helper |
| Do a relaxing before-bed routine (for example, take a hot shower, brush my hair, turn off electronics, pet my cat, listen to soothing music). | ☐ All the time ☐ Sometimes ☐ Never | ☐ Hazard ☐ Helper |

**In Bed and Waiting for Sleep to Come**

| Listen to relaxing music. | ☐ All the time ☐ Sometimes ☐ Never | ☐ Hazard ☐ Helper |
|---|---|---|
| Think about all the homework I have for the week. | ☐ All the time ☐ Sometimes ☐ Never | ☐ Hazard ☐ Helper |
| Worry about the test that I'll take the next day. | ☐ All the time ☐ Sometimes ☐ Never | ☐ Hazard ☐ Helper |
| Count sheep to relax. | ☐ All the time ☐ Sometimes ☐ Never | ☐ Hazard ☐ Helper |
| Keep my cell phone in or near my bed so I don't miss any texts or messages. | ☐ All the time ☐ Sometimes ☐ Never | ☐ Hazard ☐ Helper |

| Behavior | How Often Do I Do This? | | Sleep Hazard or Helper? |
|---|---|---|---|
| **In Bed and Waiting for Sleep to Come Back** | | | |
| Use the time to review the schoolwork and tests coming up for the week. | ☐ All the time ☐ Never | ☐ Sometimes | ☐ Hazard ☐ Helper |
| Do slow deep breathing exercises to fall back asleep. | ☐ All the time ☐ Never | ☐ Sometimes | ☐ Hazard ☐ Helper |
| Tell myself that it's normal to wake up sometimes and that I'll fall back asleep. | ☐ All the time ☐ Never | ☐ Sometimes | ☐ Hazard ☐ Helper |
| **Out of Bed in the Morning** | | | |
| Hit the snooze button several times before getting up. | ☐ All the time ☐ Never | ☐ Sometimes | ☐ Hazard ☐ Helper |
| Wait for my mom or dad to come tell me to get up several times. | ☐ All the time ☐ Never | ☐ Sometimes | ☐ Hazard ☐ Helper |
| Wait for my mom to let the dog into my bedroom to wake me. | ☐ All the time ☐ Never | ☐ Sometimes | ☐ Hazard ☐ Helper |
| Inhale the smell of breakfast cooking to help me get out of bed. | ☐ All the time ☐ Never | ☐ Sometimes | ☐ Hazard ☐ Helper |
| Fight with my parents and leave the house in a bad mood. | ☐ All the time ☐ Never | ☐ Sometimes | ☐ Hazard ☐ Helper |

| During the Day (at School and After School) | | |
|---|---|---|
| Drink caffeinated beverages or eat sugary snacks. | ☐ All the time ☐ Sometimes <br> ☐ Never | ☐ Hazard <br> ☐ Helper |
| Exercise. | ☐ All the time ☐ Sometimes <br> ☐ Never | ☐ Hazard <br> ☐ Helper |
| Plan my after-school time in order to finish homework at least one hour before I plan to go to bed. | ☐ All the time ☐ Sometimes <br> ☐ Never | ☐ Hazard <br> ☐ Helper |
| Resolve conflicts with family and friends before bedtime. | ☐ All the time ☐ Sometimes <br> ☐ Never | ☐ Hazard <br> ☐ Helper |
| Do homework in bed. | ☐ All the time ☐ Sometimes <br> ☐ Never | ☐ Hazard <br> ☐ Helper |
| Take a long nap after school. | ☐ All the time ☐ Sometimes <br> ☐ Never | ☐ Hazard <br> ☐ Helper |
| Skip the after-school nap and use this time to relax or complete homework. | ☐ All the time ☐ Sometimes <br> ☐ Never | ☐ Hazard <br> ☐ Helper |
| Eat healthy meals and snacks and avoid caffeine and sugar. | ☐ All the time ☐ Sometimes <br> ☐ Never | ☐ Hazard <br> ☐ Helper |

# more to do

Are there sleep hazards or helpers in your sleep story that were not listed? What are they?

_____

_____

_____

_____

Describe the chapters of your sleep story that may contribute to your poor sleep.

_____

_____

_____

_____

Which sleep hazards are you willing to change or at least consider changing?

_____

_____

_____

_____

## for you to know

Good sleep is essential for your physical and emotional health and well-being. There are many things that you may not know about sleep and how to manage it. One of the first steps in achieving good sleep is to learn the facts about what helps and hinders sleep.

This exercise will test your sleep IQ and review some of the facts and fallacies about good sleep.

## for you to do

Let's see what your sleep IQ is, using the following quiz. If necessary, cover the answers before you begin.

1. Jasper set his alarm for 7:00 a.m. He fell asleep at 2:00 a.m. He hit the snooze button six times and finally got out of bed at 7:30 a.m. How many hours of sleep did Jasper get?

   _____

2. Kalea drinks a caffeinated energy drink when she gets out of school at 3:00 p.m. and another one at 7:00 p.m. because she has a ton of homework. How long will the effects of the caffeine last?

   _____

3. Jake likes to do his homework in bed on his laptop and then watch Netflix until he feels tired enough to fall asleep. He knows that he's tired because he has been sleepy all day, yet he can't seem to fall asleep when he's ready. Frustrated, he texts

his friends and watches shows until well after 2:00 a.m. What late-night activities may be affecting Jake's wish to fall asleep when he's ready to sleep?

_____

_____

_____

4.  Kristin wakes up every morning feeling groggy. Is this grogginess that she experiences first thing in the morning a sign that she hasn't had enough sleep?

   a.  Yes

   b.  No

5.  More than 30 percent of high school students report falling asleep at school.

   a.  True

   b.  False

6.  What is the best strategy for combating daytime sleepiness?

   a.  Drink caffeinated beverages.

   b.  Take an hour-long nap when you get home from school.

   c.  Get outside in the sunlight and increase your activity level during the school day.

   d.  All of the above.

7.  Improving your sleep can help you eat healthier and lose weight.

   a.  True

   b.  False

8. Getting more sleep increases your attractiveness.

    a. True

    b. False

9. Getting more sleep will help you improve your grades.

    a. True

    b. False

10. Sleep deprivation causes as many accidents as drunk driving.

    a. True

    b. False

11. Zara stays up late studying for an important test. Michael chooses to study until a reasonable bedtime so he can get a good night's sleep before the test. Who is more likely to perform better on the test?

    a. Zara

    b. Michael

12. Koji had a hard time getting more than five to six hours of sleep per night during the week. So, he "caught up" on sleep over the weekend by sleeping till noon. Is Koji going to feel rested and rejuvenated on Monday morning when he needs to wake up for school? Why?

    _____

    _____

    _____

# Answers

1. Jasper got five hours of sleep. Once you awaken enough to hit the snooze button, you're snoozing, not sleeping. Snoozing doesn't give you the healthful benefits that come from real sleep. Jasper would have been better off setting his alarm clock for a more realistic 7:30 a.m. and getting thirty more minutes of true sleep!

2. Longer than you might imagine! Think of caffeine as having a six-hour half-life. That is, it takes about six hours for half of the caffeine you consume to be eliminated from your body, and another six hours for half of the remaining caffeine. So even the energy drink that Kalea consumed at 3:00 p.m. will affect her ability to fall asleep at a reasonable bedtime such as 11:00 p.m.

3. All of Jake's bright screens, and even the overhead lights in his room, are a powerful signal to his mind and body that it's time to be awake rather than to sleep. Just like sunlight, the light from computer and phone screens suppresses your body's production of the sleep hormone melatonin, which naturally induces sleepiness after dark.

4. Well, Zara thinks the answer is yes, so she starts her day feeling discouraged and tired. But actually, it's normal to feel groggy when you're waking up in the morning. Transitioning from sleeping to being awake is more like a dimmer switch than a traditional "on-off" switch. It takes time for your mind and body to move all the way from sleepiness to wakefulness. Exposing your eyes to light, listening to music, and making and eating breakfast, or simply sitting up in bed, can shorten that time. So instead of pulling the covers over your head, fling open those shades or turn on the lights and put on some upbeat music to overcome that sleep inertia!

5. True. And if you tend to fall asleep at school, you're 75 percent more likely to use caffeine to combat your fatigue, which will make it harder for you to sleep when you're ready to sleep at bedtime. Caffeine influences how long it takes you to fall asleep, how well you sleep, and how long you sleep. Because caffeine stays in your system for so long (see number 3), we recommend you try to reduce your

caffeine intake throughout the day and to not consume any at all if you'd like to fall asleep within the next six hours.

6. C. The best way to feel less sleepy is to increase your exposure to sunlight and to get your body moving, which turns on wakefulness. Try this experiment the next time you're feeling sleepy at school: rather than snoozing through chemistry or reaching for a latte, go outside and run a lap, or just run up and down the school stairs a few times. It really works!

7. True. When teens are sleep-deprived, they're more likely to crave sugary and fatty foods that can cause those unwanted pounds to stick around.

8. True. Sleep scientists have found that your peers will find you more attractive when you have slept well and enough. Yet another reason to try to get some extra z's!

9. True. Sleep deprivation impairs your ability to concentrate, solve problems, and come up with new ideas. Not surprisingly, improving your sleep can actually improve your grades.

10. True. According to the National Highway Safety Administration, drowsy driving accounts for more than 100,000 car accidents annually. In fact, sleep-deprived drivers exhibit symptoms of impairment very similar to drivers who have been drinking alcohol.

11. Michael. Memory, recall, and concentration all improve when you're rested. Staying up an extra three or four hours to cram for an exam is actually less likely to improve your grade than going to bed at a time that'll allow you to get adequate sleep. So skip the all-nighter, and get some sleep before tests and performances.

12. No. More than likely, Koji is going to feel worse on Monday morning when it's time for him to wake up, because by sleeping in, he reset his internal clock to wake up at noon (as he did on Saturday and Sunday). Koji is going to feel a grogginess very similar to jet lag!

Now take a look at your sleep IQ test. How did you do? Did anything surprise you?

_____

_____

_____

# more to do

As you're learning by now, certain things you do (or don't do) get in the way of sleep coming when you're ready to sleep. Other things you might do can help pave the way for sleep. Yet it can be hard to tell the difference, and some things that seem to help in the short term are actually insomnia traps. That is, if they become a part of your daily routine, they can trap you in the vicious cycle of trying to get to sleep only to end up lying in bed awake, worried, and frustrated.

Take a look at the following list of behaviors. Then refer to what you wrote in activity 2, when you labeled the details of your sleep story with **X**'s and **O**'s. Try to find something in your sleep story that fits with each behavior. Did you put an **X** or **O** by it? If not, or if you can't find a match, indicate whether you think the behavior is a sleep hazard (**X**) or sleep helper (**O**). (Do this now, before you read any further.)

| Behavior | | X/O |
|---|---|---|
| 1. | Drinking caffeinated beverages or consuming chocolate less than 6 hours before bedtime. | |
| 2. | Assuming that because you feel groggy in the morning, you must have had a rough night's sleep or not be rested enough. | |
| 3. | Staying up late to cram for exams. | |
| 4. | Hitting the snooze button to catch a few more minutes of sleep again and again. | |
| 5. | Eating sugary or fatty foods to stay awake or fight off drowsiness. | |
| 6. | Watching TV or videos in bed. | |

All done? Then check out how *any* of these behaviors can harm your ability to fall asleep and stay asleep night after night.

1.  It takes about six hours for half the caffeine you consumed to leave your body. This means that the caffeine in the chocolate you ate while doing homework at 7:00 p.m. could keep you awake when you're ready to sleep at 11:00 p.m. And if you have a taste for dark chocolate, you should know that it has more caffeine than milk chocolate.

2.  Everyone feels groggy in the morning because of sleep inertia. If you assume the groggy feeling means that you didn't get enough sleep, you'll worry about your sleep, and worry can make it hard to relax when night falls. It may also convince you to go to bed earlier than necessary, when you're not really tired enough to fall asleep yet.

3.  It's better to get a good night's sleep before an exam. A well-rested brain will help you concentrate and recall the information you studied. Also, during sleep, your brain will organize the information you studied and link it to your existing knowledge so that you can make better connections during the exam.

4.  Snoozing is not the same as sleeping. Repeatedly hitting the snooze button keeps your brain somewhat awake. So you'd get better rest if, going forward, you set your alarm for the time when you actually need to be up out of bed.

5.  High-sugar or high-fat foods at bedtime excite your brain at a time when you want your brain to downshift to allow sleep to come.

6.  Watching a TV or other electronic screen in bed disrupts your sleep because the light signals your brain to stay awake, and what's on the screen may be interesting and exciting, making it difficult for your mind to settle down at bedtime.

What other insomnia traps are you or your friends caught in? Which insomnia traps are strategies you used because you thought they helped you get to sleep?

_____

_____

_____

# your family's sleep story    5

## for you to know

What does your family have to do with your sleep? Well, teens who have sleep problems often come from families in which someone else has sleep problems too. We inherit our particular brain sleep patterns (night owl versus morning lark) and how much sleep we need, as well as how easily our sleep is disrupted. We can't change these things. However, there are many things you inherited that you can change, such as your beliefs about sleep and the ways you try to get sleep to come. Your family's sleep story can give you some ideas of ways to improve your own sleep, and if your family members pay attention to the adjustments you're making, they may learn to improve their sleep too.

## for you to do

Family sleep stories are made up of two main characters—the sleep attitudes and actions of every member of the family. There's not much you can do about your and your family members' general sleep appetites. Sleep appetites change across the life span. Babies have a hearty sleep appetite and typically require between sixteen and twenty hours of sleep per night. Children require as much as ten hours of sleep per night, whereas teens hunger for eight to nine hours of sleep per night (and seldom get it). As we age, our sleep appetites decrease. Adults' sleep appetites are usually seven to eight hours per night, and older adults may require even less. Some people require ten hours of sleep, and other people require six or sometimes fewer hours of sleep. Sleep appetites are hardwired, and everyone's needs are different. For example, just because your sister requires nine hours of sleep to function effectively doesn't mean that *you* do. But some families have a "one size fits all" approach when it comes to sleep. Do any of the following attitudes about sleep ring a bell when it comes to your family?

"The early bird gets the worm."

"Why sleep if you can be _____ [fill in the blank with your family's favorite activities]?"

"I'm a wreck if I don't get enough sleep."

"I don't remember ever losing a job because I didn't sleep well."

"Sleep is very important and a priority for our family."

"Sleep is important, but _____ [work, school, sports, etc.] is more important."

"We're terrible sleepers. Everyone in our family can't sleep."

"Oh well, I'll sleep better tonight because I didn't sleep well last night."

List the sleep attitudes you've heard your family members share with you or other people. Does everyone in your family have the same attitude about sleep? If not, do some attitudes conflict with other attitudes in your family?

_____

_____

_____

_____

_____

_____

What is your family's sleep motto? For example, "Sleep is for losers" or "Sleep to live well, and live well to sleep."

_____

Does your family's sleep motto support or conflict with your goal to improve your sleep?

_____

_____

_____

# more to do

Because different family members may have different sleep appetites, as well as different times when they hunger for sleep (for example, early versus late in the evening), this can create problems with your sleep.

In the following chart, list your family members, their sleep appetites (in hours), and when they generally go to bed and awaken. Start with yourself (Me).

| Family Member | Sleep Appetite (hours) | Standard Bedtime | Standard Wake-Up Time | Typical Number of Hours of Sleep | Frequency with Which Family Member Awakens Refreshed |
|---|---|---|---|---|---|
| Me | | | | | ☐ Never<br>☐ Often<br>☐ Always |
| | | | | | ☐ Never<br>☐ Often<br>☐ Always |
| | | | | | ☐ Never<br>☐ Often<br>☐ Always |
| | | | | | ☐ Never<br>☐ Often<br>☐ Always |
| | | | | | ☐ Never<br>☐ Often<br>☐ Always |

What did you notice by considering the sleep needs of each of your family members? Are there any significant differences among family members when it comes to sleep appetite, bedtime, and wake-up time?

_____

_____

_____

Describe what you learned about your family sleep story that may help you achieve your goal of sleeping better.

_____

_____

_____

Although your family sleep story may not be great, it's not necessary that you continue to live your family's sleep story. You can learn, through this book, the skills to rewrite your sleep story.

Describe the attitudes and actions that are part of your family's sleep story that you would like to change for yourself.

_____

_____

_____

# 6 getting ready to change

## for you to know

If you're struggling with insomnia, you know that sleep doesn't come easily anymore. In fact, you've likely been doing the same things over and over to get to sleep, and now these attempts to get to sleep have become unhelpful sleep habits. Changing a habit— any habit, but particularly a sleep habit—isn't easy. It takes work and, most importantly, a willingness to make difficult changes in the way you've been doing things.

However, believe it or not, you won't change your unhelpful habits just to sleep better. You'll do it to achieve what is deep and important inside you. This is the core of who you are. These are your core values. Taking time to identify your core values will help you stay on track as you begin to change your deeply ingrained sleep habits.

> Kara's family went to her grandmother's lake house every summer. She and her cousins would swim from her grandmother's dock to a beach across the lake. The beach had a buoy with a red flag on it that Kara could see from her grandmother's dock. Kara noticed that each time she set her sights for the flag and began to swim toward it, when she stopped to check her progress she would be slightly off course and she would have to redirect herself toward Red Flag Beach.

Imagine that the red flag in this story represents something that was important to Kara, such as her relationship with her grandmother. This helps illustrate what core values are and how they work. Your core values are the things that give you a sense of well-being and fulfillment, the things that influence your decisions, or the things that signify what you wish to stand for and who you wish to be. They help you determine where you want to go in life and remind you of your goals, even when you inevitably drift off course, as Kara did whenever she swam toward the beach.

# for you to do

Think back to the last scene of the *Wizard of Oz*. As Dorothy and her friends—the Lion, the Scarecrow, and the Tin Man—say good-bye to each other, the Wizard honors their unique core values—what it is they wanted the most. For the Lion, it's courage. For the Scarecrow, it's intelligence. For the Tin Man, it's love, and, for Dorothy, it's family or home.

Imagine that you're standing there with Dorothy too. What would the Wizard imply your core value was? To help uncover your core values, think about how you choose to spend your time and how the people who know you best would describe you. For example, do you spend hours talking on the phone to your friends and always find a way to help them with their problems? Would your peers say that you're caring and supportive? If so, then *friendship* is probably one of your core values.

If you have a passion for drawing or music, maybe *creativity* is one of your core values. If you practice your free-throw shots over and over, maybe *personal achievement* is one of your core values.

In the following chart, place a check mark next to the five things you value most, or the qualities you wish to be known for, in each area of your life. Feel free to add other things or qualities you value.

## Family and Friends

- ☐ Dependability
- ☐ Loyalty
- ☐ Honesty
- ☐ Helpfulness
- ☐ Harmony
- ☐ Fun
- ☐ Other: _____
- ☐ Other: _____

## School/Sports/Work

- ☐ Achievement
- ☐ Excellence
- ☐ Teamwork
- ☐ Leadership
- ☐ Knowledge
- ☐ Curiosity
- ☐ Other: _____
- ☐ Other: _____

## Play and Creativity

- ☐ Imagination
- ☐ Uniqueness
- ☐ Freedom
- ☐ Innovation
- ☐ Harmony
- ☐ Beauty
- ☐ Other: _____
- ☐ Other: _____
- ☐ Other: _____

## Health and Well-Being

- ☐ Balance
- ☐ Calmness
- ☐ Endurance
- ☐ Fitness
- ☐ Self-reliance
- ☐ Self-care
- ☐ Self-improvement
- ☐ Other: _____
- ☐ Other: _____

# more to do

Now that you know what's most important to you in several areas of your life, consider how your poor sleep habits might be harming what you hold dear. For example, if you identified **Harmony** with your family and friends as a core value, how does your insomnia affect your relationships? Does your insomnia make you irritable and impatient with your mom, your dad, and your pals? If **Imagination** and **Achievement** are core values for you, how does your insomnia affect your ability to do well in school or in a play or concert? Are you more foggy-headed after a rough night's sleep? Do you make more mistakes after not sleeping well? Jot down some notes. Then think about how changing your sleep habits might aid you in pursuit of your core values.

_____

_____

_____

_____

_____

_____

_____

# 7 setting sleep goals

## for you to know

To change your sleep story from a nightmarish tale of sleeplessness, worry, and frustration to a feel-good story that you love to curl up with every night, it's important to set some goals. When setting any goal, and particularly good sleep goals, it's essential that you take an honest and realistic look at where you are and where you want to get to.

## for you to do

Do you have any specific sleep goals not covered in the following list? If so, add them at the bottom.

| Rank | Sleep Goal | Activity Numbers |
|---|---|---|
| | Get _____ hours of sleep per night. | 6–31 |
| | Go to bed earlier. | 10–13 |
| | Fall asleep earlier or more quickly. | 6–13 |
| | Stay asleep after I fall asleep. | 19, 20 |
| | Wake up on time. | 18–22 |
| | Wake up earlier. | 21, 22 |

|  | Wake up later. | 23–27 |
|---|---|---|
|  | Have more restful sleep. | 6–31 |
|  | Worry less about sleep and other things. | 28–31 |
|  | Have fewer conflicts with my parents about sleep. | 6–31 |
|  | Feel more rested and energetic during the day. | 23–27 |
|  | Feel less sleepy during the day. | 23–27 |
|  | Other: |  |
|  | Other: |  |
|  | Other: |  |

Which goal is most important to you right now? Write a 1 in the left-hand column (Rank). Which is the next most important? Give that one a 2. Keep going, until you reach 5. These are your five sleep goals.

In the right-hand column are the numbers of specific activities in this book that can help you achieve each goal. You'll want to try all the activities in the book, but know that at any time you can go directly to the activities that seem most relevant to your goals.

# more to do

Before you start to track your progress toward your goals, make several copies of the following form (or download it from http://www.newharbinger.com/41245) to use over a period of two weeks.

| my progress toward my sleep goals | | | | |
| --- | --- | --- | --- | --- |
| **Date:** _____ | | | | |
| | Progress Toward Goal Today | | | |
| Goal 1 | 0 | 1 | 2 | 3 |
| Goal 2 | 0 | 1 | 2 | 3 |
| Goal 3 | 0 | 1 | 2 | 3 |
| Goal 4 | 0 | 1 | 2 | 3 |
| Goal 5 | 0 | 1 | 2 | 3 |
| **Date:** _____ | | | | |
| | Progress Toward Goal Today | | | |
| Goal 1 | 0 | 1 | 2 | 3 |
| Goal 2 | 0 | 1 | 2 | 3 |
| Goal 3 | 0 | 1 | 2 | 3 |
| Goal 4 | 0 | 1 | 2 | 3 |
| Goal 5 | 0 | 1 | 2 | 3 |

1. As you work through the book, circle the number that reflects your progress each day (where 0 = no progress and 3 = fantastic progress) toward the five goals you identified in the first part of this activity.

2. At the end of two weeks, review your progress forms. Did you meet some goals better than others? What might be helping or hindering your progress?

_____

_____

_____

_____

_____

_____

# 8  a good sleep attitude

## for you to know

Here's the good news. Sooner or later, sleep arrives. That's what our brains do—they sleep. Thanks to millions of years of evolution, your mind knows how to sleep, and it doesn't need your help to do it. The bad news is that sleep comes when sleep is ready to come, and the best that you (or any of us) can do is stay out of sleep's way so that it arrives quickly and easily. This is what it means to have a "good sleep attitude"—doing *less* when you're desperate to do whatever you can to get to sleep.

Think of having a good sleep attitude as accepting the fact that sleep will come when you're ready for it, versus trying to *control* when sleep will come.

Trying to control exactly when sleep comes is a bit like having your fingers in a Chinese finger trap. The more you fight to free your fingers from the trap, the more tightly the trap closes. With insomnia, the more you try, try, try to *get* to sleep, the more you push sleep away. It's counterintuitive, for sure, but once you learn and accept a good sleep attitude, you'll be on your way to better sleep.

## for you to do

Tonight, stay awake all night while you lie in bed in the dark.

Right now, you might be thinking, *That's what I do every night. How can this experiment help?* Well, it may be true that many nights you've lain awake in the dark, but on those nights you were *trying* to sleep, not trying *not* to sleep.

Give it a try. If it sounds like torture, then whenever you have a thought like one in the first column, try replacing it with one from the second column. You'll still be awake, but at least you'll be relaxed.

| Sleep-Controlling Thought | Sleep-Acceptance Thought |
|---|---|
| *I can't stand this!* | *It's okay to be awake. I know what it's like. I'll survive.* |
| *I've got to get to sleep and right now.* | *I'll rest my body while my mind is awake. That's okay.* |
| *I can't handle another minute of being awake.* | *I can stay awake all night. I know what that's like. It's okay.* |
| *This is torture. It's horrible that I can't sleep.* | *I can be at peace while I'm awake at night.* |

Wait until morning to read and answer the following questions.

What did it feel like to try to stay awake rather than trying to go to sleep?

_____

_____

_____

Did you stay awake all night?          Yes          No

Which sort of thoughts seemed to help keep you awake—those in the "Sleep-Controlling" column or those in the "Sleep-Acceptance" column? Which thoughts, if any, seemed to make you sleepy? Place a star next to those thoughts that increased your sleepiness, or write them on the following lines.

_____

_____

_____

Those thoughts that seemed to make you most sleepy—and you should include the last thought you had before you fell asleep—are your new Good Sleep Attitude phrases. Insomnia is mostly about trying to control something that you can't really control—falling and staying asleep. Change your attitude toward sleep and practice sleep acceptance rather than sleep control by saying a Good Sleep Attitude phrase to yourself from time to time as you're lying in bed each night.

# more to do

Here's another experiment to help you develop a good sleep attitude. This time, you'll try to accept that you'll awaken in the middle of the night.

| Sleep-Controlling Thought | Sleep-Acceptance Thought |
| --- | --- |
| *I hope I don't awaken in the middle of the night. I hate it.* | *It's okay to awaken in the middle of the night. I know what it's like.* |
| *I've got to stay asleep.* | *My body is resting even if my mind awakens at night. It's okay.* |
| *I can't handle awakening after I've been asleep. It's terrible.* | *I can handle awakening at night. I know what that's like. It's okay.* |
| *It's horrible to think I might not sleep well.* | *I can be at peace with the thought that I might awaken tonight.* |

Wait until the morning to read and answer the following questions.

What did it feel like to accept that you might awaken at night?

_____

_____

_____

Did you awaken in the middle of the night?               Yes          No

Describe how a good sleep attitude can help you sleep better and worry less about insomnia. How much of your insomnia is due to trying to *get* to sleep rather than waiting for sleep to come? How might you apply an attitude of acceptance to other things that you can't control but try to control anyway?

_____

_____

_____

# 9 customizing your sleep environment

## for you to know

Human beings have always been sensitive to their surroundings. In fact, a safe and secure nighttime environment was essential to our early ancestors' survival. In prehistoric times, falling asleep or sleeping for too long in the wrong kind of environment could lead to disaster: you might be eaten. This is the reason we feel more comfortable and sleep better in some environments and less comfortable and sleep worse in others.

A good night's sleep depends on a good sleep environment, and making small changes to your sleep environment can lead to big changes in your sleep.

## for you to do

Look at your sleep environment (most likely your bedroom) and identify what features of your environment or what nighttime conditions might be creating sleep hazards. You can start by considering whether your bed is comfortable. Circle the option that makes the sentence true for you. Then read why this might indicate a sleep hazard and to get some recommendations. You may be surprised to learn how your sleep environment may be disruptive to your sleep.

_____ My bed **is/isn't** comfortable.

If it **isn't:** An uncomfortable bed can make it difficult to go to sleep or can nudge you awake when you turn over. In addition, your covers may not keep you warm enough, or they may make you too warm. Comfort is a preference. You may prefer a firm or soft mattress. You might prefer warm or cool bedding. You may prefer a particular kind of pillow (firm or squishy). A new mattress may help, but a less expensive "topper" for your mattress might help too.

_____ I **do/don't** have relaxing activities (for example, Sudoku or crossword puzzles, fun books) near my bed.

If you **don't:** Focusing on a fun but relaxing activity is a good way to wind down and set yourself up for a good night's sleep. Restful activities engage your mind and delay sleep worries too. However, if you're already settled into bed, you might reach for your phone, rather than a book, if that's what's handy. So keep relaxing activities (that don't involve screens) within arm's reach.

_____ I **can/can't** dim my bedroom light or block out the light coming from my bedroom windows.

If you **can't:** Before electricity, our sleep environments were dark, except perhaps for a flickering fire. Darkness or dimness tells your brain that you're ready for sleep. Light, on the other hand, tells your brain to stay awake and stay active. Dimming or darkening your sleep environment sends the right signal to your brain: _I'm ready to sleep._ So consider installing a dimmer for your overhead light, drape a scarf over the lamp on your bedside table to dim the room while you're winding down for sleep, or install light-blocking shades in your bedroom windows.

_____ My bedroom temperature is **cool/warm** at night.

If it's **warm:** A _cool_ sleep environment tells your brain to downshift toward sleep. It's really the difference between the room temperature and your core body temperature that signals the downshift, so a super-hot shower or soak just before bed and a very cool bedroom will give you the biggest difference between room and body temperature. Also, if you're too warm, you may awaken in the middle of the night and then have trouble falling back asleep.

_____ My bedroom **is/isn't** quiet at night.

If it **isn't:** Turn on a fan, or play soft restful background music. Speak to your parents about placing carpets on wooden floors near your room.

_____ My pets **do/don't** sleep with me in bed.

If they **do:** Perhaps your cat likes to sleep on your head, or your dog twitches as he chases rabbits in his sleep. Pets snore, fidget, and jump in and out of bed, just as people do. Sleeping with your pets might not be a sleep hazard for you at all, but you might want to consider a trial period of sleeping alone to see whether your sleep improves.

_____ I **do/don't** have an alarm clock in my room.

If you **don't:** An alarm clock does not produce bright light that is a hazard for a good night's sleep. Use an alarm clock rather than your phone.

If you **do:** Turn the clock around or place it so that you can't see the time from your bed. Sleep can't tell time and doesn't really care whether it's 11:00 p.m. or 2:00 a.m. Checking the time only makes you anxious, which increases your wakefulness.

_____ I **do/don't** take my phone with me to bed.

If you **do:** Electronic devices, like phones, tablets, and laptops, produce bright light and interesting activities and images that excite your brain, so we recommend that you avoid them for at least two hours before lights-out. And make sure you can't see or hear alerts on your devices after you go to bed. If you're liable to be awakened by a text message at 2:00 a.m., you risk having trouble going back to sleep.

_____ My room is **neat and clean/dirty and disorganized.**

If it's **dirty and disorganized:** An uncluttered and nicely organized room gives your mind a break. That's because having things put away or out of sight is less likely to trigger worries about unfinished business and things like getting ready for school in the morning. Your room doesn't have to be as neat as your mom or dad may like, but a bit less clutter will tell your brain it's time to sleep.

Now look over the list. Any time your answer indicated a sleep hazard that you're able and willing to change to a sleep helper by following the recommendation, place a check mark next to it. If your answer indicated a sleep hazard that seems as though it would be very difficult to change, place a star next to it.

# more to do

Look at the sleep hazards that you marked with a star. What is it about making a change in that aspect of your sleep environment that you don't like or think wouldn't work for you? Perhaps you can't imagine how you might change it. These are just problems to be solved. On the following lines, write what you could do to solve each problem.

For example, if you don't have a dimmer switch, you can ask your parent to install one. Or, if your bedroom is disorganized because your earbuds or jewelry are on the floor or lost in a mess on the bedside table, you could mount some inexpensive wall hooks on which to hang them up neatly. Or, if your bedroom is not quiet because it's near the busy living room, you can turn on a fan to drown out the noise, or you can place rugs on any bare floors to dampen the sound.

_____

_____

_____

_____

_____

# 10 good foods for good sleep

## for you to know

Understanding the ways that foods affect your sleep can help you make good choices about what you eat and drink. For example, it's a fact that certain foods are high in tryptophan, an amino acid that helps your body produce serotonin and melatonin, chemical messengers that promote sleep.

In this activity, you'll learn which foods are good for sleep—and why—and which foods tend to push sleep away, leaving you tossing and turning in bed throughout the night.

## for you to do

Let's see what you already know about foods and sleep. Circle the best answer to each of the following eighteen items, and then check your answers at the end.

1.  Salty snacks (for example, chips or popcorn) are likely to cause you to either (a) drink too many liquids and have to pee in the middle of the night or (b) awaken in the middle of the night because you're thirsty.

    True            False

2.  _____ are rich in magnesium, a mineral that helps you stay asleep.

    Almonds            Cashews            Peanuts            Pistachios            Walnuts

3.  _____ are a good source of tryptophan.

    Almonds            Cashews            Peanuts            Pistachios            Walnuts

4. Honey is a natural sugar that gently increases your level of insulin and allows tryptophan to enter your brain more easily.

   True            False

5. Dairy products are high in calcium, which triggers the sleep-inducing chemical melatonin.

   True            False

6. Drinking soda before bed can awaken you from your sleep with an insulin jolt because of a sugar rush.

   True            False

7. Low-sodium _____ can boost your blood sugar and insulin levels, helping sleep come more quickly.

   popcorn              peanuts              pretzels

8. _____ naturally boost your levels of melatonin.

   Bananas          Cherries          Kiwis          Pears          Persimmons

9. This snack is likely to jolt you awake in the middle of night with a rush of insulin or make it difficult for you to settle down at bedtime.

   Cheese and crackers          Cookies and ice cream          Pretzels and peanut butter

10. Jasmine rice is a complex carbohydrate that produces a natural spike in your blood sugar and insulin levels, helping sleep come more quickly.

    True            False

11. _____ is **not** high in tryptophan.

    Cheese          Egg          Tofu          Turkey

12. Complex carbohydrates (breads, cereals, pasta, crackers, etc.) rapidly increase your serotonin levels, helping sleep come more quickly.

    True          False

13. A bowl of low-sugar cereal with milk is a great bedtime snack because it combines two good sleep components (carbohydrates and calcium).

    True          False

14. _____ are high in vitamin $B_6$, which your body needs to make melatonin.

    Almonds          Cashews          Peanuts          Pistachios          Walnuts

15. _____ tea contains high levels of Harman alkaloids, natural chemicals that make you feel relaxed and sleepy.

    Black          Chamomile          Earl Grey          Green          Passion fruit

16. Tuna is high in vitamin $B_6$, which your body needs to make both serotonin and melatonin.

    True          False

17. A cup of _____ tea increases your levels of glycine, a chemical that relaxes your nerves and muscles and is a mild sedative.

    black          chamomile          Earl Grey          green          passion fruit

18. Hummus is a great bedtime snack because it contains chickpeas, an excellent source of tryptophan.

    True          False

## Answers

1. True. Awakening at night may not be a problem if you go back to sleep quickly. However, if you often have difficulty falling back asleep, you should avoid salty snacks that might make you thirsty enough to get up for a glass of water in the early hours.

2. Almonds. When your body's magnesium levels are too low, it's hard to stay asleep.

3. Walnuts. Tryptophan is a sleep-enhancing amino acid that helps your body make serotonin and melatonin, the "body clock" hormone that sets your sleep-wake cycle.

4. True. A spoonful of honey in a cup of chamomile tea is a comforting and tasty route to a more restful sleep.

5. True. Dairy products, such as cheese, are a great before-bed snack to release melatonin naturally.

6. True. Soda, even diet soda, releases glucose quickly into your bloodstream. This shot of glucose awakens your brain and delays sleep.

7. Pretzels. Pretzels and also corn chips have a high glycemic index. After eating them, you'll have a natural spike in your blood sugar and insulin levels, shortening the time it takes you to fall asleep. Normally, you want to keep your sugar and insulin levels steady to avoid mood swings, but if you're looking for ways to bring sleep more quickly, the increase in blood sugar and insulin helps tryptophan enter your brain to bring on sleep.

8. Cherries. A glass of cherry juice could help you fall asleep faster. Cherries, particularly tart cherries, naturally boost melatonin levels to bring on sleep more quickly.

9. Cookies and ice cream. The simple sugars in candy, cookies, soda, and ice cream cause your body to release a big spike of glucose into your bloodstream. Because

57

your brain loves glucose and consumes a lot of it, high-sugar snacks at bedtime turn on your brain at a time when you want your brain to downshift in order for sleep to come. Even sugar-free sodas can disturb your sleep, so watch out for those too.

10. True. Rice has a high glycemic index, so eating it for dinner will significantly decrease the time it takes you to fall asleep. Jasmine rice is even more sleep-inducing than other types of rice, and it tastes great too.

11. Cheese. The calcium found in dairy products such as cheese, yogurt, and milk helps your brain use the tryptophan found in these dairy products to manufacture melatonin.

12. False. Complex carbohydrates increase your serotonin levels slowly and can delay the arrival of sleep.

13. True. Low-sugar cereal with whole milk is a great before-bed snack. Low-sugar granola and yogurt is also great.

14. Pistachios. Not only are the unsaturated fats found in peanuts, cashews, and pistachios good for your heart, but pistachios are particularly good for your sleep because of the vitamin $B_6$ that's needed to manufacture melatonin in your brain.

15. Passion fruit. Drinking a cup of passion fruit tea one hour before bed may help you sleep more soundly.

16. True. Tuna, halibut, and salmon are all high in vitamin $B_6$, which your body needs to manufacture melatonin and serotonin. Garlic is also high in vitamin $B_6$; therefore, broiled salmon with lemon and garlic tastes great and sets up your brain to sleep well.

17. Chamomile. A cup of chamomile tea before bed acts as a mild sedative.

18. True. Hummus is a great source of tryptophan, so hummus and whole-grain crackers is a wise choice of snack before bed or while you're doing homework.

Now take a look at your answers. Which of the listed foods are sleep enhancers, and, of that list, what are the foods that you like?

_____

_____

_____

_____

_____

# more to do

Now that you've learned some things about good sleep foods, list the good sleep food combinations that you already eat and drink. For example, low-sodium peanut butter on whole-grain crackers is a great combination; so is an apple with mozzarella string cheese, a banana with lowfat yogurt, or honey with a cup of chamomile tea. Yummy!

_____

_____

_____

_____

_____

# 11 dealing with unfinished business

## for you to know

Worry can motivate you to think through a problem and develop a solution for it. At the right time and in the right place, worry can be productive. But often worry comes at night when you're in bed, especially when you haven't had a moment to think about the things that are bothering you. There are so many ways of distracting yourself during the day or keeping your brain busy with other matters that bedtime might be the first time that things seem to have slowed down enough for your brain to work on the problems it wants to wrestle with. The issue with that is by then you're mentally fatigued, there's no one to talk to for help, and you end up lying awake in bed thinking through an endless string of troubling possibilities. If you have difficulty sleeping because of worry, dealing with your day's unfinished business in advance can help sleep come.

# for you to do

For this activity, make a copy of the following worksheet (or download it from http://www.newharbinger.com/41245).

| my unfinished business worksheet | |
|---|---|
| Date: _____ | |
| Concern | Solution |
| | |
| | |
| | |
| | |

Instead of letting worry creep into your sleep time, take proactive steps to deal with the day's unfinished business.

*Step 1:* Several hours before bed, when you're still alert and clear-headed, set aside ten minutes and list in the Concerns column all the problems you're dealing with that might keep you awake at bedtime.

*Step 2:* For each concern, write in the Solutions column the first step you might take to solve the problem. This may not be the final solution to the problem, because people solve most problems in steps anyway, so just write your best guess.

If you know how to solve the problem completely, write that solution. (For example, "I'll ask Mr. Samuel whether I can get some extra credit to bring my grade up.") If you decide that the concern isn't really a big problem and that you'll just deal with it when the time comes, then write that. (For example, "I'll wait to see my progress report next week before I speak to Mr. Samuel.") If you decide you just don't know what to do about the problem but can ask someone to help you, write that. (For example, "I'll ask Janie whether she did anything to bring up her grade in Mr. Samuel's class.") Last, if you decide that there isn't a good solution at all, and that you'll just have to live with the problem, write that down. Add a note to remind yourself that sometime soon you or someone you know will give you a clue that'll lead to a solution. (For example, "There isn't any solution to this problem. I bet I'll learn something tomorrow or the next day that could solve the problem, but in the meantime, I'll just live with it.")

*Step 3:* Fold the worksheet in half, and set it on the nightstand next to your bed. Tell yourself to forget about it until bedtime.

*Step 4:* At bedtime, if you begin to worry, tell yourself that you've dealt with your concerns already in the best way you know how. Remind yourself that you'll work on those concerns again tomorrow and that nothing you can do right now, when you're tired, can help you any more than what you already did earlier, when you were mentally sharp. In fact, revisiting your concerns at this time will only make matters worse by making it harder for you to sleep.

# more to do

Make more copies of the blank worksheet and use it for a couple of nights.

Then take some time to figure out the typical concerns that come up for you at bedtime. Knowing what tends to bug you at night—whether it's misunderstandings with your friends, disagreements with your parents, or difficulties with a particular school subject, such as math or history—can help you more quickly identify your concerns and think of solutions going forward.

_____

_____

_____

Describe how much easier or more difficult it was for you to relax at bedtime using this new way of dealing with your unfinished business. Do you think you'll continue to use it?

_____

_____

_____

# 12 screen diet

## for you to know

As mentioned in activity 1, electronic screens get in the way of sleep. Just the same as if you eat too many chips and drink too much soda there's a greater chance that your skin will break out, if you consume too many hours of screens during the day there's a greater chance that your insomnia will break out and that you'll lie in bed awake, frustrated, and worrying. If you really and truly want to improve the quantity and quality of your sleep, you need to go on a bit of a screen diet.

## for you to do

The first step in any diet is to monitor what and how much you consume. Monitoring your screen use will give you the information you need to create a screen-use plan that's both effective and realistic.

For this activity, make seven copies of the following form (or download it from http://www.newharbinger.com/41245).

## my screen-time log

Date: _____

| Time | Device, Location, and Activity | Minutes Used | Importance of This Activity to Me | Am I Willing to Reduce or Eliminate This Screen Time? |
|---|---|---|---|---|
| 5:00 a.m. | | | ☐ High<br>☐ Medium<br>☐ Low | ☐ Yes<br>☐ Maybe<br>☐ No |
| 6:00 a.m. | | | ☐ High<br>☐ Medium<br>☐ Low | ☐ Yes<br>☐ Maybe<br>☐ No |
| 7:00 a.m. | | | ☐ High<br>☐ Medium<br>☐ Low | ☐ Yes<br>☐ Maybe<br>☐ No |
| 8:00 a.m. | | | ☐ High<br>☐ Medium<br>☐ Low | ☐ Yes<br>☐ Maybe<br>☐ No |
| 9:00 a.m. | | | ☐ High<br>☐ Medium<br>☐ Low | ☐ Yes<br>☐ Maybe<br>☐ No |
| 10:00 a.m. | | | ☐ High<br>☐ Medium<br>☐ Low | ☐ Yes<br>☐ Maybe<br>☐ No |
| 11:00 a.m. | | | ☐ High<br>☐ Medium<br>☐ Low | ☐ Yes<br>☐ Maybe<br>☐ No |

| Time | Device, Location, and Activity | Minutes Used | Importance of This Activity to Me | Am I Willing to Reduce or Eliminate This Screen Time? |
|------|-------------------------------|--------------|-----------------------------------|-------------------------------------------------------|
| Noon | | | ☐ High <br> ☐ Medium <br> ☐ Low | ☐ Yes <br> ☐ Maybe <br> ☐ No |
| 1:00 p.m. | | | ☐ High <br> ☐ Medium <br> ☐ Low | ☐ Yes <br> ☐ Maybe <br> ☐ No |
| 2:00 p.m. | | | ☐ High <br> ☐ Medium <br> ☐ Low | ☐ Yes <br> ☐ Maybe <br> ☐ No |
| 3:00 p.m. | | | ☐ High <br> ☐ Medium <br> ☐ Low | ☐ Yes <br> ☐ Maybe <br> ☐ No |
| 4:00 p.m. | | | ☐ High <br> ☐ Medium <br> ☐ Low | ☐ Yes <br> ☐ Maybe <br> ☐ No |
| 5:00 p.m. | | | ☐ High <br> ☐ Medium <br> ☐ Low | ☐ Yes <br> ☐ Maybe <br> ☐ No |
| 6:00 p.m. | | | ☐ High <br> ☐ Medium <br> ☐ Low | ☐ Yes <br> ☐ Maybe <br> ☐ No |
| 7:00 p.m. | | | ☐ High <br> ☐ Medium <br> ☐ Low | ☐ Yes <br> ☐ Maybe <br> ☐ No |

| Time | | | High / Medium / Low | Yes / Maybe / No |
|---|---|---|---|---|
| 8:00 p.m. | | | ☐ High ☐ Medium ☐ Low | ☐ Yes ☐ Maybe ☐ No |
| 9:00 p.m. | | | ☐ High ☐ Medium ☐ Low | ☐ Yes ☐ Maybe ☐ No |
| 10:00 p.m. | | | ☐ High ☐ Medium ☐ Low | ☐ Yes ☐ Maybe ☐ No |
| 11:00 p.m. | | | ☐ High ☐ Medium ☐ Low | ☐ Yes ☐ Maybe ☐ No |
| Midnight | | | ☐ High ☐ Medium ☐ Low | ☐ Yes ☐ Maybe ☐ No |
| Total minutes used: _____ | | | | |

For one week, keep a log of your screen time across the day. Be sure to note the device you use, where you use it, and what you're doing on it. At the end of the week, calculate your daily average screen time and write it below.

_____

What did you learn from monitoring your screen time? Did anything surprise you?

_____

_____

_____

Have you ever tried to reduce your screen time before? What did you do, and how well did it work?

_____

_____

_____

_____

_____

_____

What's your average screen time during the school week versus on the weekends?

_____

_____

_____

Are there any screen activities that you might give up or cut back on to try to improve your sleep? Are there any screen activities you do close to bedtime that you could do earlier in the day instead?

_____

_____

_____

# more to do

Now that you've monitored your screen time, create a screen-use plan and test it to see whether a new plan improves your odds of getting a good night's sleep.

*Jasper created a screen-use plan that he thought might work for him. Like most things in life, it involved making a few sacrifices, but Jasper believed he could live with them if it helped him get a good night's sleep.*

| jasper's screen-use plan | |
|---|---|
| 1. | *During the week, don't check the Internet, go on social media, or play video games until I finish my homework.* |
| 2. | *Use screens after I finish my homework but not within 30 minutes of bedtime.* |
| 3. | *Put screens "to bed" outside of my bedroom so they don't wake me in the night.* |
| 4. | *Use a manual alarm clock and not my phone to awaken me in the morning.* |

For this activity, make a copy of the following worksheet (or download it from http://www.newharbinger.com/41245).

| my screen-use plan |
|---|
| 1. |
| 2. |
| 3. |
| 4. |
| 5. |
| 6. |

In the worksheet, write several guidelines to help you limit your screen use. Try the plan for three or four nights and then rate how well you were able to follow it, on a scale from 0 to 10 (where 10 = extremely well): _____ .

What did you notice on the days that you successfully followed your plan, particularly regarding evening and in-bed screen use?

_____

_____

_____

_____

_____

_____

What was the hardest part of your plan to remember? What was the hardest to actually do? What part(s) of your plan are you 90 percent confident that you'll continue to do?

_____

_____

_____

_____

_____

# 13 creating a wind-down routine

## for you to know

It's the day of the big game, and you're about to head onto the field. But there's a problem—you don't feel ready to play. Your mind is all over the place, and your body seems sluggish. *How can I possibly play well when I feel like this?* you wonder.

Then you do some stretches and practice your moves. Before long, the blood is flowing to your muscles once again and they feel loose and strong. Your attention is better focused, and you're more confident you have what it takes to compete. You're committed to giving it your best shot. By the time you finish your exercises, your mind and body have gotten the signal loud and clear—it's time to get out there and do your thing already.

A warm-up routine helps prepare your mind and body for action. It says *All right! Let's do this!* At the end of the day, however, you need a wind-down routine to prepare your mind and body for sleep, a routine that says *All right, let's go to bed.* If the things you do in the evening seem to keep you keyed up, you need to start moving in a different direction after dark. Creating a wind-down routine that you practice every night is a simple and effective way to ease your mind from daytime activities toward sleep.

A good wind-down routine is one that incorporates several things you personally find calming.

*Rachel sips warm chamomile tea out of a special mug and listens to instrumental music before she turns out the light. She does this only at bedtime, so that her mind associates the soothing fragrance of the tea, the warm feeling of the mug in her hands, and the gentle rhythm of the music with sleep. She also has a soft plush pillow that she curls up with only at bedtime. She has practiced her wind-down routine every night for three months, and now she can feel her body and mind relax the moment she smells the chamomile tea steeping in the special mug.*

# for you to do

It's important that your wind-down routine be simple yet include activities that'll signal all your senses (sight, hearing, taste, smell, and touch) that it's time to downshift and prepare for sleep.

Following are some wind-down strategies teens have said they use.

"Take a warm bath or shower."

"Close the curtains and/or dim the lights."

"Listen to calming music that I play only at bedtime."

"Stretch gently for ten minutes."

"Listen to a guided relaxation recording."

"Meditate for ten minutes."

"Breathe slowly and deeply for ten minutes."

"Sip a cup of herbal tea that I drink only at bedtime."

"Massage my face and hands with a scented lotion that I apply only at bedtime."

"Curl up in my warm bed and savor the good things that happened during the day."

"Say a wind-down mantra to myself for five minutes (for example, 'silver moon,' 'cobalt night,' 'easy sleep')."

"Turn off any screens in my room."

"Write in my journal the good things that happened during the day."

1. Come up with a few of your own wind-down strategies. Just remember that the goal is to wind your mind down, not up. For example, it may seem relaxing to sit on the couch and watch your favorite drama or thriller, but an exciting storyline or spooky music can get you mentally pumped.

   _____

   _____

   _____

2. Which of the strategies above—including the examples—would you consider trying every night for two weeks? Underline them. Which strategies don't suit you, aren't doable, or would be difficult to remember? Cross them out.

3. Try three or four of the strategies over the next couple of weeks and then decide whether they helped. Place a check mark next to the ones that helped and an **X** next to the ones that didn't. Write down your thoughts as to why these strategies did or didn't help you.

   _____

   _____

   _____

# more to do

Now that you've identified several wind-down strategies that might work for you, it's time to create a personalized wind-down routine and see how it works. Here's an example.

| rachel's wind-down routine | |
|:---:|:---|
| 1. | *Set my alarm and turn the clock around so that I can't see it from my bed.* |
| 2. | *Close the curtains and/or cover the light above my bed with a transparent scarf to dim the light.* |
| 3. | *Write a few thoughts about my day, particularly things I might wish to savor later.* |
| 4. | *Listen to my "Calming Music" mix while I massage my hands with lotion.* |
| 5. | *Brush my hair gently 20 times.* |
| 6. | *Hold the mug of chamomile tea while I close my eyes and inhale its fragrance for 1 minute.* |

For this activity, make a copy of the following worksheet (or download it from http://www.newharbinger.com/41245).

| my wind-down routine | | | | | | |
|---|---|---|---|---|---|---|
| Start Date: | | | | | | |
| Strategy 1: | | | | | | |
| Mon. _____ | Tue. _____ | Wed. _____ | Thu. _____ | Fri. _____ | Sat. _____ | Sun. _____ |
| Strategy 2: | | | | | | |
| Mon. _____ | Tue. _____ | Wed. _____ | Thu. _____ | Fri. _____ | Sat. _____ | Sun. _____ |
| Strategy 3: | | | | | | |
| Mon. _____ | Tue. _____ | Wed. _____ | Thu. _____ | Fri. _____ | Sat. _____ | Sun. _____ |
| Strategy 4: | | | | | | |
| Mon. _____ | Tue. _____ | Wed. _____ | Thu. _____ | Fri. _____ | Sat. _____ | Sun. _____ |
| Strategy 5: | | | | | | |
| Mon. _____ | Tue. _____ | Wed. _____ | Thu. _____ | Fri. _____ | Sat. _____ | Sun. _____ |
| Strategy 6: | | | | | | |
| Mon. _____ | Tue. _____ | Wed. _____ | Thu. _____ | Fri. _____ | Sat. _____ | Sun. _____ |

1. In the worksheet, write three to six wind-down strategies, to compose a routine you can spend twenty to thirty minutes doing.

2. Try the routine for one week, using all the strategies each night (in any order you wish). Each day, at the bottom of the worksheet, using a scale from 0 to 5 (where 5 is extremely well and 0 is not well at all), rate how well the wind-down routine helped prepare your mind and body for sleep.

3. Make more copies of the blank worksheet, and try several different routines until you find one that really and truly works for you.

4. Look at the different wind-down routines that you tried. Which routine did you like the most? Which one worked the best? Which one worked the least?

_____

_____

_____

_____

_____

_____

Most teens find that a wind-down routine helps their minds and bodies prepare for sleep. However, it takes practice and time—sometimes several weeks—before your mind begins to settle into a new and different way of getting ready for sleep. So the best wind-down routine is the one that you're most likely to use every night.

# 14 slow deep breathing

## for you to know

Slow deep breathing is a great activity to try while lying in bed at night. Not only does slow deep breathing give you something to do while waiting for sleep to come, but also it combats any stress and worry about when and how well you'll sleep.

## for you to do

Slow deep breathing is easy. To practice it, just follow three simple steps:

*Step 1:* Close your eyes and imagine you have a red balloon attached to the end of a long tube that starts in your nose and ends in your stomach. Place your hand on your stomach (over your navel), and feel how that balloon inflates and deflates in rhythm with the rising and falling of your stomach as you breathe.

*Step 2:* Keep your hand resting on your stomach, and inhale slowly and deeply through your nose as you count to three. Pause and hold your breath for another count of three, and then slowly exhale through your mouth. Imagine the red balloon inflating as you inhale and deflating as you exhale. Take another slow, deep breath in through your nose as you count to three. Hold it for one-two-three, and release for one-two-three. Pause for a moment and then inhale, one-two-three. Hold for one-two-three, and exhale for one-two-three. Pause.

*Step 3:* Say to yourself *Calm* and visualize the word "calm" using your mind's eye as you inhale for one-two-three. Hold that breath for one-two-three, and then say to yourself *Mind* and visualize the word "mind" as you exhale one-two-three. Repeat: Inhale, *Calm*, one-two-three. Hold, one-two-three. Exhale, *Mind*, one-two-three. Pause.

Practice this way of breathing for two to three minutes at first. Over time, see whether you can do it for longer, until you reach five to ten minutes. To track your practice, you can download My Slow Deep Breathing Log from http://www.newharbinger.com/41245. If your mind wanders as you practice this way of breathing for longer periods, just refocus your attention on the picture of the word ("mind" or "calm") in your mind's eye and continue inhaling and exhaling, slowly and deeply.

Now that you're good at slow deep breathing, try it while waiting for sleep to come (or waiting for sleep to come *back* after you wake up in the night). What did you notice? Did you feel a bit less stressed about when sleep would come? Did sleep come a bit more quickly when you were practicing slow deep breathing?

_____

_____

_____

# more to do

Now that you've learned slow deep breathing, you can use it to decrease your stress and worry during the day so that you're less stressed and less worried at bedtime.

List a few events or situations that tend to cause you to worry (for example, taking an exam, friends pressuring you to take sides, speaking with a teacher, and doing homework).

_____

_____

_____

Select a couple of stressful events or situations that tend to happen a lot at home or at school. Jot them down in the following worksheet. Close your eyes, take some time to imagine yourself in one of these situations, and then rate your stress level on a scale from 0 to 10 (where 0 = completely relaxed and 10 = highly stressed). Then, practice slow deep breathing for five minutes and re-rate your stress level.

| Stressful Event or Situation | Stress Level *Before* Deep Breathing | Stress Level *After* Deep Breathing |
|---|---|---|
|  |  |  |
|  |  |  |
|  |  |  |
|  |  |  |

Describe what it was like to breathe deeply and slowly as you imagined a stressful event or situation. How quickly did you feel relaxed and calm? Did you learn anything else that might be helpful?

_____

_____

_____

# progressive muscle relaxation 15

## for you to know

Stress, particularly daily stress, causes your muscles to become more and more tense, and this muscle tension can make it difficult for sleep to come at bedtime. Progressive muscle relaxation is an easy-to-learn exercise that can help you relax your body fully and release the tension that keeps you tossing and turning in bed. Not only does progressive muscle relaxation help you release your body's tension, but also it's a great activity to do while waiting for sleep to come.

## for you to do

Read the following script (steps 1 to 5) aloud and record it on your phone or another device. Then listen to the recording in bed at night to help you practice tensing and relaxing various muscle groups. (Or there may be an app or online recording you can use. Search for "guided PMR.")

Before you give this new way of relaxing a whirl, find a quiet place and get into a comfortable position. Loosen any tight clothing so that you can breathe easily. Then follow these steps.

1. Squeeze your eyes tight, scrunch your nose as if you're smelling a rotten egg, pull the edges of your mouth back toward your ears into a forced smile (like you're experiencing g-forces), and bite down to tense your mouth and jaw. Count slowly to fifteen. Then slowly relax your eyes, nose, mouth, and jaw for another fifteen seconds. Relax your face so that all the wrinkles disappear and your face is smooth and relaxed, your cheeks feel soft, and your tongue is loose in your mouth. Notice how different this feels from when your face was tight and tense.

2. Tuck your neck into your shoulders like a scared turtle. Hold this position for fifteen seconds, observing the pull on your neck muscles and the discomfort you feel. Now release, and let your shoulders drop down and relax your head. Hold for fifteen seconds.

3. Make fists with your hands and cross your arms at the wrists. Hold your arms up in front of you and push them together as if you're arm-wrestling with yourself. Maintain this position with your fists clenched for fifteen seconds. Then let your fists uncurl and your arms slowly fall to your side. Hold this position for fifteen seconds.

4. Suck in your stomach, making your abdomen get hard and tight, and clench your buttock muscles. Hold this position for fifteen seconds. Notice the uncomfortable tension. Then release and let your stomach go out further and further while you relax your buttock muscles. Do this for fifteen seconds. (You might notice as you go through all of these muscle exercises, tensing and relaxing, that you're starting to feel more relaxed.)

5. Tighten your leg muscles by pointing your toes straight out and bending your ankles back toward you. While holding this position, curl your toes into a tight ball. Hold for fifteen seconds and then release for fifteen seconds. Your legs might feel loose and floppy as they begin to relax.

To relax your body even more, repeat the steps, beginning again with your facial muscles. To track your practice, download My Progressive Muscle Relaxation Log from http://www.newharbinger.com/41245.

# more to do

Progressive muscle relaxation is only one of many strategies you can use to relax your body and increase your ability to handle stress. For example, exercise—even just a short walk around the block—is a great stress-reducer. Some teens find that taking a hot bath or shower relaxes their bodies, particularly at bedtime, when it can help downshift the mind and body so that sleep comes quickly and easily.

What are your favorite ways to relax your body?

_____

_____

_____

Describe how you feel and how well you sleep after you do your favorite relaxing activity.

_____

_____

_____

_____

_____

_____

_____

# 16 savoring

## for you to know

To savor means to enjoy something deliberately and slowly, such as you might inhale the aroma of a warm chocolate chip cookie and then take only a small bite at first, to make the pleasurable experience last as long as possible. You can savor memories too, particularly memories of feeling happy or comfortable, such as the time you won a soccer game or the time you spent a fun day at the beach with your friends.

Savoring a memory is another great activity to try while waiting for sleep to come. Not only does savoring give you something to think about while waiting for sleep to come, but also it creates pleasant feelings that combat stress and worry about when and how well you'll sleep.

## for you to do

List three good times you had recently (for example, fun activities, favorite places you've visited, good times you've shared with friends or family, or successes in your life).

1. _____

2. _____

3. _____

Pick one of the good times from your list, and picture it in your mind. Try to remember everything about the event—where you were and when it happened, who you were with, and how you felt. Answer the following questions to help you identify the elements of the story.

Where were you, and what was happening? What did you hear, smell, and see?

_____

_____

_____

How did you feel (for example, happy, proud, satisfied, joyful, and loved)?

_____

_____

_____

What was going through your mind when you were feeling the good feelings?

_____

_____

_____

What was your role in shaping this good time? How did you set it up or help make it happen?

_____

_____

_____

Imagine that this good time leads to more good times and good feelings in the future. What would that look like?

_____

_____

_____

Now that you've created a story about your good time and good feelings, read through it again. Finally, close your eyes and savor your good time by replaying your story in your mind.

Rate the intensity of the recollection—the mental images, sounds, smells, and so forth— and the intensity of the good feelings you feel on the following scale:

| Intensity of Recollection | 1 | 2 | 3 | 4 | 5 |
|---|---|---|---|---|---|
| Intensity of Good Feeling | 1 | 2 | 3 | 4 | 5 |

Now that you've learned how to savor a pleasant memory, try savoring tonight while you wait for sleep to come. The next morning, in the space below, describe what that was like.

_____

_____

_____

# more to do

You can also try the savoring activity to relax, calm down, and interrupt the worry spiral that can occupy your mind once you lie down to wait for sleep to come. To break the escalating cycle of worry at bedtime, practice shifting back and forth between worrying and savoring.

1. Think of a situation or concern that you're worrying about a lot. It might involve your friends, school, your family, your health, or anything else. Give yourself complete freedom to worry about the situation for about two minutes.

2. Savor for two minutes one of the happy memories you listed in the first part of this activity. Remember to think about all the elements of the story (for example, where you were and when it happened, who you were with, and how you felt).

3. Resume worrying for two minutes. Then go back to savoring for two minutes. Do this a few times.

Try it tonight while you wait for sleep to come—keep shifting between worrying and savoring. In the morning, describe what it was like.

Did you feel more calm and relaxed while lying in bed?

_____

_____

_____

Did it help with the worries you had about how quickly sleep would come?

_____

_____

_____

To see whether savoring to relax works better over time, make a copy of the following form (or download it from http://www.newharbinger.com/41245) and use it for a week as you savor a pleasant memory each night. Put a mark in the column that corresponds to how well savoring worked to relax you, where 10 means you were extremely relaxed and 0 means you were not relaxed at all.

| my savoring to relax log | | | | | | | | | | | |
|---|---|---|---|---|---|---|---|---|---|---|---|
| Start Date: _____ | | | | | | | | | | | |
| | How Well Did Savoring to Relax Work? | | | | | | | | | | |
| **Night** | 0 | 1 | 2 | 3 | 4 | 5 | 6 | 7 | 8 | 9 | 10 |
| Sunday | | | | | | | | | | | |
| Monday | | | | | | | | | | | |
| Tuesday | | | | | | | | | | | |
| Wednesday | | | | | | | | | | | |
| Thursday | | | | | | | | | | | |
| Friday | | | | | | | | | | | |
| Saturday | | | | | | | | | | | |

# for you to know

Meditating doesn't mean emptying your mind or keeping your mind completely still, and anyone can do it. You can use meditation to shift your attention away from the things that stress you or make you anxious.

Here's one way to think about meditation. Imagine a ship anchored in a harbor, at rest. The ship is not going anywhere, even though it's not exactly still—it moves up and down with the waves. Because even when a big wave rolls into the harbor and begins to carry the ship with it, the anchor pulls the ship back to the same spot.

Just like a ship, your mind is capable of taking you all over the map. Learning to meditate simply involves finding a quiet place to cut the engines and focusing your attention on an anchor amid the waves of thoughts and feelings that'll arise, so that you keep coming back to the same restful spot. Your anchor can be anything you choose— you may want to focus on the movement of your chest as you breathe, a continual sound such as a clock ticking, a word you chant aloud or to yourself, or a peaceful and neutral image. In meditation, an anchor is just something calming to remind yourself of when your attention inevitably drifts. No matter how far your thoughts or emotions carry you from your anchor, you can shift your attention back to it and resume bobbing in place on the gentle waves of your breath.

Meditation is a terrific "waiting for sleep to come" strategy. It's relaxing, and it can help you unhook from sleep worry or the frustration of lying awake when you'd rather be dreaming. Also, with practice, you can learn to shift your attention quickly even when you're not meditating, which can help you stay calmer in stressful situations throughout the day.

*Wendy's older sister, Gabby, returned home from her first year of college looking and sounding different. She said that college was super-stressful, but she had taken a meditation class that helped a lot. Over dinner, Gabby explained how meditation was catching on all over the country as something that anybody could do. She said, "Tibetan monks aren't the only people meditating these days." She said that learning to meditate was difficult at first but that over time she was able to meditate for longer and longer.*

*Wendy didn't say much to Gabby about it, but she was interested, and, that night, in her bedroom, she tried meditating. She sat on her bed and closed her eyes and focused her attention on a mental image of the big white flower on the magnolia tree outside her window. She realized quickly that her sister was right: meditation was not easy. However, she managed it for thirty seconds a couple of times that night, and after a few weeks she was meditating for five minutes and then for ten minutes. After several more weeks she started to notice that she felt more relaxed during the day and that she was sleeping better. Also, and this surprised her the most, she was focusing better in her classes. That helped a lot because school was the most stressful part of her life.*

# for you to do

Coming up with your personal anchor can be fun.

Circle the words that feel the most relaxing to you.

| | | | |
|---|---|---|---|
| Flower | Ocean | Peace | Sunset |
| Tree | Sky | Summer | Moon |
| Mountain | Water | Sleep | Quiet |
| Free | Clouds | Love | Relax |
| God | Home | Friendship | Calm |

Come up with some relaxing words of your own.

_____

_____

Select one of the words you circled or wrote to focus on during your first meditation practice. Find a quiet place and sit or lie down in a comfortable spot. Close your eyes, and silently repeat the word to yourself. As you repeat the word, visualize a calming image that goes with it. For example, if the word is "moon," visualize a beautiful full moon on a warm and quiet night. Focus your attention on the word and the mental image.

How did the meditation feel?

_____

_____

_____

What did you like about the meditation?

_____

_____

_____

What did you *not* like about the meditation?

_____

_____

_____

# more to do

Develop a plan to practice meditation regularly. Decide on a time and place to meditate that works for you. Would you prefer to meditate in the morning or in the evening? Is your room the best place to meditate, or is there a spot outside you would enjoy? We recommend that you begin with short practice periods, perhaps one minute each day.

_____

_____

_____

Put your plan into action. Try to meditate for one or two minutes at first and then, as you feel ready (for example, at one-week intervals), increase the length of your meditations by one or two minutes until you're practicing regularly for ten to fifteen minutes at a stretch. This might take three or four weeks, but select a pace that works for you.

# your lights-out plan 18

## for you to know

Once you've given your body time to relax and wind down, it's time to turn off the light, settle under the covers, and wait for sleep to come. This crucial part of the night—lights-out—is often stressful for teens with insomnia. They've spent months and sometimes years trying to make sleep come, and when it doesn't come right away, they begin to worry whether sleep will come at all.

Creating a lights-out plan can help you relax a bit before waiting for sleep to come. Remember, sleep will come if you stay out of sleep's way, and having a lights-out plan can help.

*Ben hasn't been sleeping well since he and his family moved to a new town at the end of his sophomore year of high school. Ben used to sleep just fine, but now after Ben turns out the light in his room, he lies in bed for two or three hours trying to get to sleep, worrying about not sleeping, and feeling more and more frustrated. It's become so bad that Ben doesn't even want to turn out the light because he knows that once he does, the worry, frustration, and sleeplessness will start.*

## for you to do

In this activity, you'll create a personalized lights-out plan and see how well it works. A good sleep attitude is the most essential part of your lights-out plan. Remember, a good sleep attitude encourages you to do *less* even when you're desperate to do whatever it takes to get to sleep.

1. Review activity 8 ("A Good Sleep Attitude") and write the Good Sleep Attitude phrases you came up with from that activity. You'll include these in your lights-out plan.

_____

_____

_____

2. Think of some things you can do while lying in bed waiting for sleep to come. Following are some strategies you can use. Place a check mark next to a strategy if you wish to include it in your lights-out plan. At the bottom, add any strategies that you've used in the past that relax you and give your mind something to do while you wait for sleep to come.

| | |
|---|---|
| Slow deep breathing (activity 15) | |
| Progressive muscle relaxation (activity 16) | |
| Savoring (activity 17) | |
| Meditation (activity 18) | |
| Listening to a guided relaxation or guided meditation | |
| Repeating a simple word or phrase (for example, "the," "hat," "milk," or "marshmallow") | |
| Counting backward from 100 | |
| Other: | |
| Other: | |
| Other: | |

Make a copy of the following worksheet (or download it from http://www.newharbinger.com/41245).

| my lights-out plan |
| --- |
| **Good Sleep Attitude Phrases** |
| **Steps** |
| 1. |
| 2. |
| 3. |
| 4. |
| 5. |
| 6. |
| How well did it work? |

| 0 | 1 | 2 | 3 | 4 | 5 | 6 | 7 | 8 | 9 | 10 |
| --- | --- | --- | --- | --- | --- | --- | --- | --- | --- | --- |

| Notes: |
| --- |
|  |

3. In the worksheet, write your lights-out strategies in the order you'd like to do them. Remember to begin with your Good Sleep Attitude phrases.

Here's Ben's lights-out plan:

| ben's lights-out plan |
| --- |
| **Good Sleep Attitude Phrases** |
| *It's okay to be awake. My body is resting while my mind is awake.* |
| *I can let go and wait.* |

| **Steps** | |
| --- | --- |
| 1. | *Repeat several times my Good Sleep Attitude phrase: "It's okay to be awake. My body is resting while my mind is awake."* |
| 2. | *Practice progressive muscle relaxation.* |
| 3. | *Count backward from 100.* |
| 4. | *Practice slow deep breathing for a few minutes.* |
| 5. | *Repeat the word "marshmallow" or "roundabout" for a few minutes while I breathe slowly.* |

4. Follow the plan as you lie in bed tonight waiting for sleep.

5. In the morning, rate how well it worked, on a scale from 0 to 10. Add your notes or observations.

# more to do

Look at the lights-out strategies that you tried in your plan.

Which one helped you relax and wait for sleep the best?

_____

What other strategies might you include in your lights-out plan?

_____

_____

_____

Create a new lights-out plan that may work better, and try it. Experiment with several different lights-out plans until you find one that works really well.

# 19 when sleep doesn't come, what then?

## for you to know

Sleep comes to those who wait, but waiting a long time while you're lying in bed isn't a good idea. If sleep doesn't come in twenty to thirty minutes, you're likely to toss and turn, worry, and try harder to get to sleep. The harder you try, the more frustrated you'll feel, and the frustration and worry will keep sleep away. After a while, your mind and body will expect that you'll feel wide awake the moment you turn out the lights.

You can break this psychological connection between being in bed and being awake (a bed-awake connection), and create a connection between being in bed and being asleep (a bed-asleep connection), by training yourself to leave your bed whenever you've been waiting at least twenty minutes for sleep to come. Doing some enjoyable, soothing activities will take some of the dread out of waiting for sleep and give your mind something to do (other than worrying) until that deliciously sleepy feeling returns.

## for you to do

It's difficult to get out of a warm, comfy bed at night if the place you'll go isn't comfortable or the things you'll do aren't soothing and at least a little enjoyable. The first step is to create a comfortable waiting place and identify and organize pleasant activities that won't amplify your wakefulness. These will be the activities you do in the waiting place.

Identify which activities in the following table are enjoyable at least sometimes. Then indicate whether those activities tend to increase or decrease your wakefulness. This is important because you won't want to use activities that'll push sleep away. For example, reading a book (a traditional book, not an e-book—remember to avoid screens at bedtime) is a great waiting activity, unless the book is a mystery and you're getting to a suspenseful part. Then you might discover that you're more awake and not even paying attention to whether you're feeling sleepy. Add any other activities that might be good for you to do when you can't sleep. Wakefulness is like a dimmer switch. Certain activities turn wakefulness up or down, so look for activities that are a little enjoyable but turn your wakefulness down. Also, if you live with others, you'll want to identify quiet activities, such as working on crossword puzzles or reading a magazine, so long as these don't involve a screen.

| Nighttime Activity | Is It Enjoyable? | | | Wakefulness | |
|---|---|---|---|---|---|
| Check e-mail. | ☐ Yes | ☐ No | ☐ Sometimes | ☐ Up | ☐ Down |
| Watch the clock. | ☐ Yes | ☐ No | ☐ Sometimes | ☐ Up | ☐ Down |
| Watch YouTube videos. | ☐ Yes | ☐ No | ☐ Sometimes | ☐ Up | ☐ Down |
| Draw on a sketchpad. | ☐ Yes | ☐ No | ☐ Sometimes | ☐ Up | ☐ Down |
| Read a book or magazine. | ☐ Yes | ☐ No | ☐ Sometimes | ☐ Up | ☐ Down |
| Play solitaire with a deck of cards. | ☐ Yes | ☐ No | ☐ Sometimes | ☐ Up | ☐ Down |
| Play solitaire or knit. | ☐ Yes | ☐ No | ☐ Sometimes | ☐ Up | ☐ Down |
| Take a hot shower or bath. | ☐ Yes | ☐ No | ☐ Sometimes | ☐ Up | ☐ Down |
| Listen to music. | ☐ Yes | ☐ No | ☐ Sometimes | ☐ Up | ☐ Down |
| Do homework. | ☐ Yes | ☐ No | ☐ Sometimes | ☐ Up | ☐ Down |
| Other: | | | | | |
| Other: | | | | | |

Look over your list of nighttime activities. What do you notice? Is there a connection between what you do at night and how awake you feel at bedtime?

_____

_____

_____

For those times when you've just gone to bed but no longer feel sleepy, it's important that you have a comfortable and calming place to go to while you wait for sleepiness to return. On the following lines, describe what items you'd like to include in this waiting place. Perhaps you want to keep a book to read or earbuds so that you can listen to soothing music on a small table near a comfortable chair. Include a warm duvet or sleeping bag to keep you warm. If there isn't room for a chair, perhaps a mattress or a couple of pillows will do.

_____

_____

_____

_____

_____

# more to do

Now that you have a comfortable place to go to and soothing activities to do while you wait to feel sleepy, put these pieces together the next time you've been lying in bed awake for what feels like more than twenty minutes. (Estimate the time rather than using a clock, because watching the clock will only add to your anxiety and frustration.) If you find yourself reluctant to get out of bed, remember that waiting in bed awake is why sleep isn't coming in the first place. Resist the urge to stay in bed another minute. Go immediately to your waiting place and do one of the activities you identified as somewhat enjoyable and calming. It doesn't matter which soothing activity you do while you wait, so long as you're doing something other than worrying. If it's getting hard to keep your eyes open, that's great—it's a sign of *sleep pressure*, your body's urge to sleep. Sleep pressure means sleep is on the way, but don't rush back to bed just yet. It's important to have enough sleep pressure, not just a little. So when you begin to feel some sleep pressure, wait for five more minutes and then return to bed. If sleep doesn't come in another twenty to thirty minutes, repeat the process.

Be patient with yourself, and stick with the strategy. It's probably taken weeks and months for you to build that bed-awake connection. It will take some time to tear it down and build a new, bed-asleep connection.

After one week:

1. Describe any connection you notice, particularly with how quickly sleep starts to come. Are you falling asleep faster than before, or at least spending less time awake in bed?

   _____

   _____

   _____

2. Do you notice any change in your level of frustration, worry, and dread?

   Yes            No

# 20 when sleep doesn't come back, what then?

## for you to know

If you're like most teens, by the time you close your eyes you're exhausted, and usually you go to sleep quickly. However, that doesn't mean you sleep through the night. Worries, including sleep worries, and poor sleep habits can cause you to wake up in the middle of the night and find it hard to fall back asleep. How many times have you lain in bed awake, tossing and turning, because the sleep that came on so effortlessly at the beginning of the night isn't coming back? It helps to have a plan to cope with this frustration when you can't get back to sleep.

## for you to do

If you're one of those teens who go to sleep easily but wake up in the night and have a tough time falling back asleep, you probably do things to try to get back to sleep quickly or to catch up on the sleep you lost during the night.

Indicate how often you've done the following things in an effort to go back to sleep or catch up on sleep. Add any others you can think of.

| I Gotta Get Back to Sleep! | |
|---|---|
| Take medicines (for example, melatonin) to aid sleep. | ☐ Often ☐ Never <br> ☐ Sometimes |
| Wear a sleep mask or earplugs. | ☐ Often ☐ Never <br> ☐ Sometimes |
| Stay in bed awake to try to get back to sleep. | ☐ Often ☐ Never <br> ☐ Sometimes |
| Tell myself, Go to sleep! | ☐ Often ☐ Never <br> ☐ Sometimes |
| Tell myself, Just a couple more minutes. Sleep is close. | ☐ Often ☐ Never <br> ☐ Sometimes |
| Repeatedly check the clock to see how long I've been awake. | ☐ Often ☐ Never <br> ☐ Sometimes |
| Other: | |
| Other: | |

| I Gotta Catch Up on Sleep! | |
|---|---|
| Get into bed earlier than normal. | ☐ Often ☐ Never ☐ Sometimes |
| Stay in bed after the alarm goes off. | ☐ Often ☐ Never ☐ Sometimes |
| Go to bed when I'm tired during the day (nap). | ☐ Often ☐ Never ☐ Sometimes |
| Follow a rigid pre-sleep routine. | ☐ Often ☐ Never ☐ Sometimes |
| On weekends, sleep 2 hours or more past my usual wake-up time. | ☐ Often ☐ Never ☐ Sometimes |
| Other: | |
| Other: | |

How many or which of these strategies have actually helped you fall back asleep faster or sleep better at night and be more productive during the day?

_____

_____

_____

How might certain strategies work against you? For example, a pre-sleep routine, such as your wind-down routine, helps you prepare for sleep. However, a wind-down routine can be unhelpful if you feel as though you must follow it to "get" to sleep. That's not a Good Sleep Attitude. What are strategies that you use to *get* to sleep? Those are the ones that work against you.

_____

_____

_____

_____

_____

_____

# more to do

Make several copies of the following form. On the left are strategies that may be more helpful than those you've already tried if you have trouble sleeping through the night. At the bottom, add any other strategies you can think of.

| my good sleep strategies log | | | | | | | |
|---|---|---|---|---|---|---|---|
| Start Date: _____<br><br>(✓ if you met your goal) | **Mon.** | **Tue.** | **Wed.** | **Thu.** | **Fri.** | **Sat.** | **Sun.** |
| Go to my waiting place if I'm awake for 30 minutes. | | | | | | | |
| No naps. | | | | | | | |
| On weekends, sleep no longer than 2 hours past my usual wake-up time. | | | | | | | |
| Get out of bed immediately when the alarm rings. | | | | | | | |
| Exercise for 10 minutes when I'm tired rather than nap. | | | | | | | |
| Only sleep in bed (no homework or hanging out in bed). | | | | | | | |
| Resist going to bed early to try to catch up on sleep. | | | | | | | |

| | | | | | | | |
|---|---|---|---|---|---|---|---|
| Remind myself that sleep has a mind of its own. It will come. | | | | | | | |
| Practice savoring while waiting for sleep to come. | | | | | | | |
| Practice slow deep breathing while waiting for sleep to come. | | | | | | | |
| Practice progressive muscle relaxation while waiting for sleep to come. | | | | | | | |
| Practice meditation while waiting for sleep to come. | | | | | | | |
| Resist using caffeine or sugar to stay alert during the day. | | | | | | | |
| Use my wake-up routine (activity 22) in the morning and other times when I feel tired. | | | | | | | |
| Other: | | | | | | | |
| Other: | | | | | | | |
| Other: | | | | | | | |

1. Pick any three of these good sleep strategies and practice them for a couple of weeks, placing a check mark in the appropriate column each day you successfully followed a strategy.

2. Pick three different ones, and practice *these* good sleep strategies for a couple of weeks. The idea is to find the good sleep strategies that work best for you. Remember, no two teens have the same sleep story, and therefore no two teens will use the same good sleep strategies.

3. Is there a connection between the quantity and quality of your sleep and whether you used good sleep strategies?

    Yes          No

4. Which strategies did you use most often? Why? Which strategies were more difficult to do? Why?

   _____

   _____

   _____

   _____

   _____

   _____

# a teen at rest tends to stay at rest 21

## for you to know

Have you ever seen a magician yank a tablecloth out from beneath plates sitting on a table? What happens to the plates? Well, when the trick works, the plates stay on the table. This is inertia. The law of inertia tells us that an object at rest tends to stay at rest. This is true for sleep too. When your mom or dad comes into your bedroom and pulls the blankets off you, your sleep stays put, like the plates on the table. This is sleep inertia.

Why should you care about sleep inertia? Well, if you confuse sleep inertia with feeling as if you didn't get enough sleep, you'll stay in bed, push the snooze button over and over, and wait to feel awake and alert before you get out of bed, which will actually make it tougher for sleep to come when you go to bed that night.

# for you to do

Here's a fun experiment that'll teach you something about your own sleep inertia.

Make a copy of the following worksheet (or download it from http://www. newharbinger.com/41245).

| my sleep inertia experiment | | |
|---|---|---|
| Start Date: _____ | My Inertia Level | |
| Monday | Getting out of bed: | |
| | 5 minutes later: | |
| | 10 minutes later: | |
| Tuesday | Getting out of bed: | |
| | 5 minutes later: | |
| | 10 minutes later: | |
| Wednesday | Getting out of bed: | |
| | 5 minutes later: | |
| | 10 minutes later: | |
| Thursday | Getting out of bed: | |
| | 5 minutes later: | |
| | 10 minutes later: | |
| Friday | Getting out of bed: | |
| | 5 minutes later: | |
| | 10 minutes later: | |

1. For the next five weekday mornings, record your degree of sleepiness (on a scale from 0 to 10, where 10 = extreme sleepiness) three times: first as soon as you get out of bed, then five minutes later, and then five more minutes later. You can ask your mom or dad to help you with this, if one of them typically wakes you up in the morning. Just have your mom or dad (or whoever wakes you up) ask you for your sleep inertia number.

2. At the end of the week, describe what you noticed. How big a change in your sleep inertia did you see?

_____

_____

_____

# more to do

Sleep inertia tends to decrease on its own the longer you're out of bed, but you can try a few things to speed up the process.

1. For the next five mornings, repeat the sleep inertia experiment. But this time when you get out of bed, try something new: go to the window, open the curtains and flap your arms up and down (or do jumping jacks) and take three deep breaths.

2. Describe what you noticed. How big a change in your sleep inertia did you see at five and ten minutes this time?

_____

_____

_____

# 22 creating your wake-up routine, really and truly

## for you to know

When you don't sleep well or don't sleep enough, it can be tough to wake up and get going in the morning. Fatigue, distress from tossing and turning all night, worry about how you'll get through the day, and the sleep inertia and sleep pressure you feel can all play a role in this. You may linger in bed, repeatedly pushing the snooze button, hoping that you'll sleep for at least a few minutes more. But as you probably know, snooze-button sleep is restless, fitful, and shallow. It's better to get up and get going, and a wake-up routine can help. In addition, during the day, when you're feeling the tug of sleep and desperately want a nap (napping can make it hard to sleep later, as we'll explore in activity 23), you can use some of the strategies in your wake-up routine to help you power through the lull.

## for you to do

No two wake-up routines are the same. Some teens use a bitterly cold shower to get themselves going. Other teens like to sing along with their favorite tunes to ease more slowly into the day.

1. Place a check mark next to any of the following strategies that have ever awakened you quickly. In addition, place a check mark next to any strategy you might want to try. Perhaps you can't imagine using a particular strategy (for example, a cold shower in the morning) or you would use a particular strategy but it's unlikely your family would be cool with it (for example, crowing like a rooster). If so, come up with your own version of the strategy and add that to the list.

| | |
|---|---|
| Take a cold shower. | |
| Open the curtains (and my eyes) and stand in sun for 2 minutes. | |
| Dance to my favorite tune for 2 minutes. | |
| Jog in place for 2 minutes. | |
| Sing at the top of my lungs for 2 minutes. | |
| Listen to my favorite tune while I pick out my clothes. | |
| Take 5 slow deep breaths and flap my arms like an eagle. | |
| Drink a cup of tea or coffee. | |
| Kick off the covers and move my arms and legs as if I'm making a snow angel in the bedsheets. | |
| Yawn loudly 5 times. | |
| Crow like a rooster or Peter Pan. | |
| Other: | |
| Other: | |

2. Tomorrow morning, try using one of these strategies.

3. Later, describe what effect it seemed to have on your day.

_____

_____

_____

_____

_____

Can you see yourself using this strategy every day as part of a wake-up routine? If not, pick another strategy from the list and give it a go.

# more to do

Now that you've identified wake-up strategies that work for you and tested one or more of them, create a personalized wake-up routine and see how well it works.

Here's an example of a wake-up routine.

| michael's wake-up routine |
| --- |
| 1. Kick off the bedcovers. |
| 2. Crow like a rooster. |
| 3. Get out of bed, stand, and take three slow deep breaths. |
| 4. Turn on some music and dance into the bathroom. |

Make a copy of the following worksheet (or download it from http://www.newharbinger.com/41245).

| my wake-up routine |
| --- |

Start Date: _____

1.

2.

3.

4.

5.

6.

7.

**How well did it work?**

| 0 | 1 | 2 | 3 | 4 | 5 | 6 | 7 | 8 | 9 | 10 |
| --- | --- | --- | --- | --- | --- | --- | --- | --- | --- | --- |

Notes:

1.  Create your wake-up routine by listing in the worksheet at least three wake-up strategies, in whatever order you think will work best.

2.  In the morning, try out this new way of starting your day. Follow the steps of your routine.

3.  Indicate how well the routine worked to wake you up, on a scale from 0 to 10. Add your notes or observations. For example, did your brother scream at you for crowing too loud? Did your parents tell you to knock it off?

4.  Create a new wake-up routine, or tweak the one you wrote so that it might work better. Then try it out the next morning.

5.  Experiment with several different routines until you find one that really and truly works for you (and your family).

## for you to know

Sleep pressure is that wonderful feeling that signals that sleep is coming. You know the feeling, particularly when you're trying to stay awake: consciousness begins to seem increasingly difficult to maintain. You feel a kind of heaviness—perhaps your eyelids grow droopy—as a pleasant fatigue spreads through your body and slows down your movements. The dream world seems to beckon, and you find it hard to concentrate. This is the way your mind and body let you know they're hungry for sleep.

As you go through your day, your mind and body begin to crave sleep. Napping feeds your appetite for sleep the same way that snacking feeds your appetite for food. Just as you don't want to ruin your appetite at mealtime by eating a snack too close to dinner, if you want sleep to come quickly at bedtime then it's essential that your mind and body remain hungry for it. That's why napping is a no-no.

This activity can help you understand how napping interferes with sleep and what you can do to nap less and sleep better.

# for you to do

Make seven copies of the following diary (or download it from http://www. newharbinger.com/41245).

| my sleep-appetite diary | | | | | | | | | | | |
|---|---|---|---|---|---|---|---|---|---|---|---|
| **Nap Today?** ☐ Yes  ☐ No | | | | | | | | | | | |
| **Length:** _____ | | **Date:** _____ | | | | | | | | | |
| **Time of Day** | **My Sleep Appetite** | | | | | | | | | | |
| **Waking Up** | 0 | 1 | 2 | 3 | 4 | 5 | 6 | 7 | 8 | 9 | 10 |
| Comments: | | | | | | | | | | | |
| **Midday** | 0 | 1 | 2 | 3 | 4 | 5 | 6 | 7 | 8 | 9 | 10 |
| Comments: | | | | | | | | | | | |
| **Homework Time** | 0 | 1 | 2 | 3 | 4 | 5 | 6 | 7 | 8 | 9 | 10 |
| Comments: | | | | | | | | | | | |
| **Bedtime** | 0 | 1 | 2 | 3 | 4 | 5 | 6 | 7 | 8 | 9 | 10 |
| Comments: | | | | | | | | | | | |

Record your level of sleep appetite at various times during the day (on a scale from 0 to 10, where 10 = you can't keep your eyes open) for the next seven days. Also, record the length of your naps (for example, one hour vs. ten minutes). But for two or three of those days, try not to nap (even briefly).

# more to do

Looking back at your completed sleep-appetite diaries:

Describe the difference in sleep appetite you felt on the days you napped compared to the days you didn't nap.

_____

_____

_____

What date and what time of day (waking up, midday, homework time, bedtime) was your sleep appetite the highest? What other times did you feel high sleep appetite?

_____

_____

_____

Describe any connection you notice, particularly at bedtime, between your sleep appetite and your nap habits.

_____

_____

_____

Are there any patterns involving your sleep appetite, the time of day, and whether you napped?

Yes          No

# 24 using caffeine and sugar to combat daytime drowsiness—not!

## for you to know

When you haven't slept well or you don't sleep much to begin with, it's only natural to look for an energy boost during the day. Most teens reach for a caffeinated beverage, such as coffee; a sugary snack, such as candy; or the powerhouse caffeine-sugar combination—soda. Let's be honest: caffeine and sugar work if your goal is to combat daytime fatigue. However, they don't work if your goal is to sleep well.

Caffeine influences how long it takes you to fall asleep, how well you sleep, and how long you sleep. Understanding the role of caffeine and sugar in pushing off sleep can help you avoid the vicious insomnia cycle in which you consume caffeine and sugar to stay awake during the day but then the caffeine and sugar make it difficult to sleep at night.

## for you to do

Make fourteen copies of the following form (or download it from http://www. newharbinger.com/41245).

| my caffeine and sugar diary | | | | | | | | | | | |
|---|---|---|---|---|---|---|---|---|---|---|---|
| Date: _____ | | | | | | | | | | | |
| Time of Day | My Drowsiness Level | | | | | | | | | | |
| Waking Up | 0 | 1 | 2 | 3 | 4 | 5 | 6 | 7 | 8 | 9 | 10 |
| What I Ate or Drank | | | | | | | | | | | |
| Midday | 0 | 1 | 2 | 3 | 4 | 5 | 6 | 7 | 8 | 9 | 10 |
| What I Ate or Drank | | | | | | | | | | | |
| Homework Time | 0 | 1 | 2 | 3 | 4 | 5 | 6 | 7 | 8 | 9 | 10 |
| What I Ate or Drank | | | | | | | | | | | |
| Bedtime | 0 | 1 | 2 | 3 | 4 | 5 | 6 | 7 | 8 | 9 | 10 |
| What I Ate or Drank | | | | | | | | | | | |

1. For the next week, drink and eat the same caffeinated and sugary foods you usually consume. Record your drowsiness level, on a scale from 0 to 10 (where 10 = can't keep your eyes open) at each time of day (waking up, midday, homework time, bedtime) and the sugary and caffeinated foods and beverages you ate and drank during or close to these times.

2. Now, for the following week, drink only one caffeinated beverage in the morning, and don't eat any sugary foods after 1:00 p.m. each day. Record your drowsiness level at the same times of day.

# more to do

Looking back at your completed caffeine and sugar diaries:

What foods did you consume during or just before the times when you rated your drowsiness as low, perhaps 4 or less?

_____

_____

_____

Describe any connection you notice, particularly at bedtime, between your level of drowsiness and the amount of caffeinated and sugary beverages and foods you consumed.

_____

_____

_____

Are there any patterns involving your level of drowsiness, the foods you consumed, and the time of day, particularly bedtime?

Yes        No

# exercising to combat daytime drowsiness 25

## for you to know

Perhaps you now see the role that caffeine and sugar play in that vicious cycle of trying to fight drowsiness during the day but paying the price at night when sleep refuses to come. "So," you might ask, "How do I combat daytime fatigue without using caffeine and sugar?" The answer is to get your body moving. Exercise helps and almost never hinders sleep.

# for you to do

Make seven copies of the following diary.

| my exercising to combat daytime drowsiness diary | | |
|---|---|---|
| Date: _____ | | |
| Time of Day | My Drowsiness Level Before Exercise<br><br>0  1  2  3  4  5  6  7  8  9  10<br><br><br>My Drowsiness Level After Exercise<br><br>0  1  2  3  4  5  6  7  8  9  10 | Exercise and Duration |
| Time of Day | My Drowsiness Level Before Exercise<br><br>0  1  2  3  4  5  6  7  8  9  10<br><br><br>My Drowsiness Level After Exercise<br><br>0  1  2  3  4  5  6  7  8  9  10 | Exercise and Duration |

For the next week, set a goal of exercising instead of consuming caffeine or sugar on two occasions when you feel drowsy (but when it's not yet close to bedtime) each day. In the diary, record the time of day you felt drowsy, your drowsiness level, and how you exercised and for how long (for example, "I jogged in place for ten minutes" or "I walked around the track three times"). Then answer the following questions.

Looking back at your completed diaries, how would you describe the difference in your drowsiness level before and after you exercised?

_____

_____

_____

Do your diaries show that exercise might work better for you than caffeine and sugar?

Yes          No

What might be some other benefits to using exercise rather than caffeine and sugar to combat daytime fatigue (for example, can it save you money or help you lose weight)?

_____

_____

_____

# more to do

If you're just starting out, the notion of exercise probably seems tedious and unrewarding. In addition, you may think you lack the discipline or the strength for it. When you think of exercise, perhaps you see yourself failing to do a push-up or collapsing on a treadmill. You're envisioning a sort of hardcore fitness training, a workout strictly for the sake of losing weight or building strength and endurance.

But there are many, many other ways to get exercise. You just need to find a physical activity that suits you. For example, if you like excitement and adventure, then maybe you can learn to skateboard or surf. If you'd enjoy being on a team with people you know, why not sign up for a sport at school? If your idea of fun is something more laidback and familiar, you might spend a sunny afternoon playing Frisbee with your brother or sister. And for some quality alone time you can always go for a long walk with your earbuds in.

You won't know whether you like a certain activity until you try it, and remember: it just might improve your sleep. Whenever you do almost any kind of physical exercise during the day, at night your mind and body will be so relaxed that sleep will come more easily. Also, exercising on a regular basis can reduce any stress and anxiety that keeps you awake at night.

1. Place a **star** next to any of the following popular physical activities that you enjoy, and **circle** any that you've never done but would like to try.

| | | | |
|---|---|---|---|
| Hiking with a friend | Playing catch | Dancing in my bedroom | Yoga |
| Swimming | Calisthenics | Rollerblading | Jogging |
| Rock climbing | Football | Dance class | Lifting weights |
| Jumping rope | Tennis | Bowling | Spin training |
| Mountain biking | Volleyball | Baseball | Karate |
| Water aerobics | Badminton | Windsurfing | Shooting baskets |
| Dance aerobics | Judo | Skateboarding | Snowboarding |
| Wrestling | Kickboxing | Surfing | Skiing |

2. Select one or two circled activities you could try in the next couple of weeks.

3. Exercising isn't always easy for busy teens. The best way to fit a bit more exercise into your day is to make time for it in your schedule. So on the following lines, write the physical activities you'll do and the days and times you'll do them. Be realistic, though; it's okay to start with a few minutes of exercise and increase it over time.

_____

_____

_____

_____

_____

_____

4. Get your body moving as planned, and then get a good night's rest!

# 26 planning your day to make time for more sleep

## for you to know

Many teens don't prioritize sleep over the many other things they could do each evening. If you don't make enough time for sleep, particularly dedicating the last part of your day to winding down and preparing for sleep using some of the activities you've learned in this workbook, then you'll end up trying to *get* to sleep as quickly as you can. That doesn't work.

As you've learned, you can't simply make yourself sleep. You can't rush around in the evening trying to do as much work or have as much fun as possible and then rush off to bed, treating sleeping as just another thing you need to or want to do. (Thinking that you can fall asleep if only you concentrate hard enough or long enough is the opposite of a good sleep attitude.) Planning your day, on the other hand, can help you finish the many important tasks you have and still leave time for sleep.

Planning your day can help you schedule sufficient time to wind down, relax, and prepare to sleep. Although planning takes a little work, it'll save you the stress and worry that come with running from one activity to the next in a chaotic way that can contribute to your insomnia. Planning your day will help you better manage your day, and this will help you sleep when you finally lie down at night.

# for you to do

Make seven copies of the following worksheet (or download it from http://www. newharbinger.com/41245).

| my planning for sleep worksheet | | | |
|---|---|---|---|
| Date: _____ | | | |
| Time | Task | Priority (A, B, C) | How Did I Do? (1, 2, 3) |
| 5:00 a.m. | | | |
| 6:00 a.m. | | | |
| 7:00 a.m. | | | |
| 8:00 a.m. | | | |
| 9:00 a.m. | | | |
| 10:00 a.m. | | | |
| 11:00 a.m. | | | |
| Noon | | | |

| | | | |
|---|---|---|---|
| 1:00 p.m. | | | |
| 2:00 p.m. | | | |
| 3:00 p.m. | | | |
| 4:00 p.m. | | | |
| 5:00 p.m. | | | |
| 6:00 p.m. | | | |
| 7:00 p.m. | | | |
| 8:00 p.m. | | | |
| 9:00 p.m. | | | |
| 10:00 p.m. | | | |
| 11:00 p.m. | | | |
| Midnight | | | |

On these worksheets, schedule all your activities (for example, homework, soccer practice, friend time, family time, after-school activities, and relaxation time) for each day of the week, *but* start by scheduling two sleep tasks—when you'll begin your wind-down routine and when you'll turn out the lights. These are priority-A (most important) tasks. Once you've scheduled those tasks (Wind-Down Time and Lights-Out), fill in everything else you need or want to do. Prioritize each task according to how important the task is to complete (A = very important, B = moderately important, and C = not at all important). Remember, the time you'll begin your wind-down routine and the time you'll turn out the lights are priority-A tasks.

Notice the shaded area from 4:00 p.m. to 10:00 p.m. This is "crunch time," when you're usually trying to cram homework, relaxation, and friend and family time into a few hours before bed. Planning and prioritizing during crunch time is particularly important. Try scheduling priority-A tasks in the earlier time slots (for example, 4:00 p.m. to 7:00 p.m.) so that the heavy stuff isn't hanging over you all evening and so that you'll be better able to wind down and relax before bedtime.

At the end of the day, rate how close you came to completing each task within the time you scheduled for it (where 1 = bull's-eye, 2 = close but no cigar, and 3 = missed the target completely). In this way, you'll fine-tune your ability to estimate the amount of time these kinds of tasks actually take. As you learn to plan more accurately, you'll feel more on top of things and better able to make time to sleep.

# more to do

After several days of creating and following the schedule, describe what it was like to plan your day in this way. Did you have more time to complete your wind-down routine? How often did you turn out the lights at the time you scheduled?

_____

_____

_____

_____

With which activities did you hit the bull's-eye, and with which activities did you miss the target completely? Which kinds of activities do you need the most help with to complete on time, and why?

_____

_____

_____

_____

If you didn't hit the bull's-eye with your wind-down routine and lights-out times, what do you think got in the way?

_____

_____

## for you to know

It doesn't matter how well you plan your day in order to make time for sleep at night—all that planning won't help if you don't get down to business. Learning to quickly start your homework, piano practice, and all the other things on your to-do list will actually add time back into your day and decrease your worry and stress. Having more time to do your wind-down routine and less worry because you've completed the things on your to-do list will make room for sleep to arrive after you've finished your work for the night.

> *Jake was a big-time procrastinator. He habitually put off doing his homework, practicing the piano, and even taking a shower before bed. Jake couldn't understand how Ben, his best friend, seemed to do things without putting them off, even things that were boring or stressful. So Jake decided to ask Ben how he did it. Ben said, "I learned long ago that it's better to tell myself to do it now than to tell myself it's okay to do it later."*

## for you to do

Teens who put things off usually bargain with themselves to get permission to do other things first. They tell themselves, *I'll start my homework after I watch this last video,* or *I'll clean my room after I finish my homework.* Putting off undesirable tasks such as homework only increases your stress and can keep you awake long past the time you'd like to be asleep. You can't help wishing to procrastinate, but if you talk back to those kinds of thoughts you can keep yourself moving on your to-do list.

Following are typical thoughts teens have that give them permission to put things off. Place a check mark next to thoughts you often have yourself. In the blanks, add any of your own typical thoughts.

| | |
|---|---|
| *I'll do it later.* | |
| *I'll do it when I know exactly how to do it.* | |
| *I'll do it when I have more time.* | |
| *I'll do it when I'm less tired.* | |
| *I'll do it after I do a little more research.* | |
| *I'll do it after I play this last video game or watch this last show.* | |
| *I'll do it in the morning on the way to school. It won't take long.* | |
| *I'll feel more like doing it tomorrow.* | |
| Other: | |
| Other: | |
| Other: | |

Often, when teens give themselves permission to put off undesirable tasks, they experience undesirable consequences like having trouble falling and staying asleep. What consequences have you experienced because you gave in to your permission thoughts and put things off?

_____

_____

_____

# more to do

Look back at your list of typical permission thoughts. For each one, what could you say that would challenge the permission thought and help you face the task? For example, in response to the permission thought *I'll write the essay after I do a little more research*, you could say, *I'll start my essay now, and as I write the essay, I'll know what more research I really need.*

Write your answers.

| Permission Thought | Move-It-Ahead Thought |
|---|---|
|  |  |
|  |  |
|  |  |
|  |  |

Getting good at challenging your permission thoughts won't happen overnight. These sorts of thoughts have probably been rolling around in your head for years. It'll take time for you to get good at not giving yourself permission to put things off. Sometimes teens feel a little stressed when they think about changing a familiar and "comfortable" pattern of procrastination.

Describe any concerns you have about giving up procrastination, and explain why.

_____

_____

_____

Imagine that you never learn to challenge your permission thoughts. In what ways might your life get harder or more stressful?

_____

_____

_____

## for you to know

There are three kinds of worries that keep teens awake. The first kind of worries are the day-to-day worries that spin through your mind when you lie down to sleep. *What if I bomb the big test tomorrow? What if Julia breaks up with me? What if I can't make friends at the new school?* These worries are tough enough to handle during the day, but when they make you restless at night, you may begin to worry about not sleeping too. This is the second kind of worry. *What if I can't sleep tonight? What if I get to sleep but wake up in a cold sweat like I did last night?* Then there's the third kind of worry. It's the double whammy of sleep worry. This is when you worry about how not getting enough sleep might affect the other things you worry about. *What if I fail my test because I'm too tired to think? What if I'm exhausted tomorrow and I blow the soccer game? What if I'm so tired in the morning that I sleep through my alarm and miss the SAT?*

In this activity, you'll learn more about your particular worries and worry patterns so that you can begin to worry less and sleep better.

## for you to do

This activity will help you identify the kinds of worries that stress you out and make it difficult for you to sleep.

Look at the following list of worries. Circle the kinds of worries you have and what your worry typically focuses on. If you often have a worry thought that's very much like an example, circle that too.

| Kind of Worry | Focus of Worry | Example Worry Thought |
|---|---|---|
| Day-to-Day Worry | Performance | *What if I flunk my exam?* |
| | Friends | *What if Jay thinks I'm weird?* |
| | Family | *What if my parents get a divorce?* |
| | Health | *What if I get diabetes because of stress?* |
| | World Events | *What if we can't stop climate change?* |
| Sleep Worry | Sleep | *What if I don't sleep at all tonight?* |
| Double-Whammy Worry | Performance | *What if I'm so tired that I can't play well?* |
| | Friends | *What if I'm so tired that my friends think I'm boring?* |
| | Family | *What if my mom lectures me about my sleep?* |
| | Health | *What if I get sick because I can't sleep?* |

Describe how it feels to recognize the kinds of worries you have. Do you see any connection between your day-to-day worries and the double-whammy worries?

_____

_____

_____

# more to do

There are your worries, and then there are the ways you handle your worry, particularly your worries about sleep.

If you've used any of the following ways of handling your worry, indicate how helpful they've been in solving your sleep problem.

| Strategy for Handling Sleep Worry | Is It Helpful? | | |
|---|---|---|---|
| I distract myself with schoolwork, gaming, TV, or other activities to get my mind off my sleep problem. | ☐ Yes | ☐ Sometimes | ☐ No |
| I use alcohol or drugs to feel better and less stressed about getting enough sleep. | ☐ Yes | ☐ Sometimes | ☐ No |
| I speak to an adult or a teacher I trust about what's stressing me. | ☐ Yes | ☐ Sometimes | ☐ No |
| I exercise a little more when I'm worried about not sleeping. | ☐ Yes | ☐ Sometimes | ☐ No |
| I eat more than usual or eat more unhealthy foods than usual when I haven't slept well. | ☐ Yes | ☐ Sometimes | ☐ No |
| I pray or meditate to relax and feel better even if I haven't slept well. | ☐ Yes | ☐ Sometimes | ☐ No |
| I accept that I can't do much about the problem and try to live with the fact that I didn't sleep well. | ☐ Yes | ☐ Sometimes | ☐ No |
| I get involved in a hobby, a sport, or other healthy things I enjoy to help myself feel better even when I haven't slept well. | ☐ Yes | ☐ Sometimes | ☐ No |
| I criticize myself when I don't perform well, even if I haven't slept well. | ☐ Yes | ☐ Sometimes | ☐ No |

| Strategy for Handling Sleep Worry | Is It Helpful? | |
|---|---|---|
| I take a little time to relax, breathe, and unwind before bedtime. | ☐ Yes ☐ No | ☐ Sometimes |
| I avoid interacting with my friends when I haven't slept well. | ☐ Yes ☐ No | ☐ Sometimes |
| I try to suppress my worries about getting enough sleep, even when I've been sleeping okay. | ☐ Yes ☐ No | ☐ Sometimes |
| I cancel appointments when I haven't slept well. | ☐ Yes ☐ No | ☐ Sometimes |
| I avoid exercising when I haven't slept well. | ☐ Yes ☐ No | ☐ Sometimes |

Describe what you learned about the strategies you use to get to sleep or handle the days when you're tired because you haven't slept well. If there are strategies that you use that actually help you worry less about getting enough sleep and don't create more problems for you, describe them and explain why they help.

_____

_____

_____

_____

_____

# for you to know

All teens worry. Some worries are helpful. When you think, *I have a B in math class now. What if I fail tomorrow's final exam?*, you're motivated to study and perhaps motivated to ask the teacher for extra help. Some worries are less helpful, such as when you think, *Last night was horrible. What if I have another night like that? If I don't get at least eight hours of sleep, I'm useless.* Whether the worry is helpful or not, a worry always starts with a thought. When you understand the situations and thoughts that trigger feelings of anxiety, you can manage worry—even the worries you already have about getting enough sleep—better. Situations, thoughts, and feelings are the A-B-C of sleep worry.

*Devon is a worrier. He has worried pretty much about everything—friendships, exams, and even his health—all his life, but recently he has started to worry about his sleep too. Most nights, he turns out his lights and starts to worry about all he has to do the next day, but one night he started to worry that if he didn't sleep enough, he might develop a serious illness. He had trouble sleeping that night, and the next day he went to the school counselor, Mr. Hayashi, for help.*

*Mr. Hayashi was surprised that Devon was so worried about his sleep, and he was very surprised when Devon shared his big worry that day. Mr. Hayashi thought it might help to teach Devon the A-B-C of sleep worry. This is what he and Devon came up with.*

| A<br><br>**A** is for antecedent, the situation that triggers your worry. | *I'm in bed and exhausted. I can't get to sleep again.* |
|---|---|
| B<br><br>**B** is for belief, the thoughts and beliefs that make you feel anxious. | *If I can't sleep and this continues, maybe this will start to affect my health. Maybe my immune system will get weak. Then I'll get sick all the time. I'll start to miss classes because I'm sick, and then I'll stress about that, and that'll affect my immune system.* |
| C<br><br>**C** is for consequence, the anxious feelings that make you uncomfortable and make it difficult for you to sleep. | *Anxious and stressed. I'm super anxious. I can't sleep, but I can't think about anything else. I'm thinking about staying home from school, and that's freaking me out too.* |

What do you notice about the circumstances surrounding Devon's sleep worry? Do you ever worry about how your poor sleep might affect your health? If not, why?

_____

_____

_____

# for you to do

Understanding the when and why of your particular sleep worries can help you let go of certain worries and handle your anxiety better on the whole.

Make several copies of the following log (or download it from http://www. newharbinger.com/41245). Over the next two weeks, when you notice that you're worried about not sleeping well, make a note in the log. (The first row gives you an example of how to fill it in.)

| my a-b-c sleep-worry log | | | | |
|---|---|---|---|---|
| Day/ Date | Time | A Situation | B What I'm Thinking | C Anxiety Level (1–3) |
| Thurs Jan. 5 | 10:00 p.m. | Getting ready for bed. | *What if I can't sleep?* | 2 |
| | | | | |
| | | | | |
| | | | | |
| | | | | |

# more to do

Looking back at your completed A-B-C sleep-worry logs for the past two weeks.

What was it like to pay attention to your thoughts?

_____

_____

Describe any patterns you notice over time. Do you have the same sleep worries most nights? What other worries do you have, other than worries about getting enough sleep?

_____

_____

_____

Describe what you learned about yourself from these sleep-worry logs.

_____

_____

_____

In what ways might paying attention to your sleep worries, and other worries, help you manage your feelings of anxiety at bedtime and throughout the day?

_____

_____

_____

# for you to know

Your thoughts don't necessarily reflect reality. They may paint an inaccurate or distorted picture of the world. Especially when you're exhausted or anxious, your brain may make incorrect assumptions or come to misleading conclusions. We call these "thinking mistakes."

If you worry too much and can't seem to stop, you're probably unaware that you're making the same thinking mistakes over and over again. In other words, things aren't necessarily as bad as you assume they are. Catching a thinking mistake can help you distance yourself or unhook your mind from unhelpful sleep worries so that you can cope and sleep better even when the worry is there. And the better you get at catching your sleep-worry thinking mistakes, the better you'll get at quickly unhooking your mind from any unhelpful worry.

# for you to do

There are many kinds of thinking mistakes that lead to sleep worry or to excessive worry in general. In this activity, we'll focus on four sleep-worry thinking mistakes most teens tend to make over and over again.

**Thinking Mistake 1: Fortune-telling.** You predict that bad things are very likely to happen, when in fact there's very little evidence a bad thing will happen at all. For example:

- *I'll fail my math test tomorrow because I didn't sleep well.*

- *I'm going to wake up tonight at two o'clock, just like last night.*

**Thinking Mistake 2: Mind-reading.** You assume that you know what your friends, your teachers, and other people are thinking and that they're thinking the worst about you, when in fact there's no evidence to support it. For example:

- *They think I'm such a loser because I missed that goal.*

- *Gloria thinks I don't like her because I'm so spacey from not sleeping last night.*

**Thinking Mistake 3: Horribilizing.** You blow things way out of proportion. Something that's bad is not just bad; it's *horrible*. For example:

- *I can't handle making a C on my math test.*

- *If I don't get enough sleep tonight, I'll feel like a wreck all day long.*

**Thinking Mistake 4: Catastrophizing.** You tend to predict the worst, rather than waiting to see how things will play out, and thus you don't get a chance to learn that, in reality, the worst doesn't happen all that often. For example:

- *This time, I'll fail my Spanish final. I won't know a single thing.*

- *If I don't get to sleep right now, I won't get a wink of sleep the rest of the week.*

Look at the following thoughts and decide whether the thought is a thinking mistake. If it's a thinking mistake, circle which kind it is.

1. *I can barely keep my eyes open. My teacher must think I don't like her class.*

   Fortune-telling   Mind-reading   Horribilizing   Catastrophizing

2. *I'm tired this morning, but so are most of my friends.*

   Fortune-telling   Mind-reading   Horribilizing   Catastrophizing

3. *I can't handle another night of tossing and turning.*

   Fortune-telling   Mind-reading   Horribilizing   Catastrophizing

4. *If I don't get enough sleep, I'll get sick and have to drop out of school.*

   Fortune-telling   Mind-reading   Horribilizing   Catastrophizing

5. *I studied all week for the math test, but I'm still unprepared. I'm going to flunk big-time.*

   Fortune-telling   Mind-reading   Horribilizing   Catastrophizing

6. *I'll probably toss and turn for a while, but in the end sleep will come.*

   Fortune-telling   Mind-reading   Horribilizing   Catastrophizing

**Answers:** 1. Mind-reading 2. Mind-reading 3. Horribilizing 4. Fortune-telling and catastrophizing 5. Fortune-telling and catastrophizing 6. No thinking mistake.

# more to do

Think back to times this past week when you were worrying about friends, school, or sleep. Write the kinds of thoughts you were having.

_____

_____

_____

_____

_____

Do the thoughts you just wrote seem to embody one or more of the four thinking mistakes—fortune-telling, mind-reading, horribilizing, or catastrophizing?

_____

_____

_____

Over the next day or two, listen closely when your friends talk about *their* sleep. Try to identify which, if any, thinking mistakes they're making. You might hear a friend say, "I couldn't fall asleep last night. It's going to be a horrible day," or "I'm never going to be able to fix my sleep." If you think you hear a thinking mistake, write down the type of thinking mistake and why you think it's a mistake.

---

---

---

---

---

# 31 decatastrophize your sleep worries

## for you to know

Many teens who don't sleep well tend to worry about the consequences of their poor sleep. They tend to blow these consequences out of proportion (that is, they catastrophize—see activity 30). To lower your sleep worry and sleep a bit better at night, you can learn to decatastrophize your sleep worries.

*Janai is freaking out about her sleep again. Tomorrow is the junior prom, and she's worried that if she doesn't sleep well, she won't be much fun at the dance. She told her mom about this worry, and her mom came back with something unexpected: "Let's say that you're tired and not much fun at the junior prom tomorrow night. Okay, and then what?" When Janai thought it through, this put the brakes on her worry.*

## for you to do

The first step in decatastrophizing your sleep worry is to identify a typical sleep worry and dig into it until you tunnel down to the worst thing imaginable, the catastrophe that keeps the entire worry process going. To do this, you state your worry and then ask yourself, *And then what?*—in other words, what could happen if your fear came true—until you arrive at the deepest negative prediction, the most frightening thing that could realistically happen.

Here's Janai's tunnel-down process:

"If I don't sleep well tonight, then I'll be tired tomorrow."

*And then what?*

▼

"I won't be much fun at the junior prom."

*And then what?*

▼

"My friends won't want to hang out with me."

*And then what?*

▼

"I'll look weird, and my friends won't want to hang out with a loser."

*And then what?*

▼

"I'll never be asked to do anything again, and I'll spend the
rest of the year and next year alone and miserable."

Wow! Janai's mind travels at the speed of light, going from worrying that she'll feel tired at the prom because she didn't sleep well to spending the rest of her time in high school rejected and alone. That's a catastrophe for sure.

Now you try.

Identify a typical sleep worry you have from time to time, and tunnel down to the catastrophe using the following worksheet. Keep asking yourself *And then what?* until you can't imagine where it might lead or what would be worse. You may want to make copies of the worksheet before you begin, to use later with other worries. You can also download it from http://www.newharbinger.com/41245.

| my tunnel down to the catastrophe worksheet |
|---|
| Sleep-worry thought: |
| ▼ |
| And then… |
| ▼ |
| And then… |
| ▼ |
| And then… |
| ▼ |
| And then… |
| ▼ |
| And then… |

Look at where you began the tunnel-down process (the sleep-worry thought), and look at where you tunneled down to. Are you surprised at the potential catastrophe that lurks in your sleep-worry thought? Describe what the tunneling-down process was like for you.

_____

_____

_____

Now, ask yourself, *If one of my friends had this thought about getting poor sleep, would I think my friend's thought was accurate?* Write your answer to the question and how that new perspective made you feel and think about your own sleep problem.

_____

_____

_____

# more to do

Thinking through how you *would* handle a catastrophe, in the unlikely event that it occurred, can decrease your anxiety about it too.

1. Write the worst thing that could happen—the potential catastrophe—from the first part of this activity.

   _____

2. How anxious do you feel (0–100, where 100 = extremely anxious) when you think about this happening?

   _____

3. Imagine it *did* happen. What can you do to recover? How might you try to solve your problems? What skills, information, or resources do you have that would help you handle the situation?

   _____

   _____

   _____

4. How anxious do you feel now (0–100, where 100 = extremely anxious) when you think about the potential catastrophe?

   _____

5. Describe how your anxiety changed in this activity. If it decreased, what do you think helped decrease it?

_____

_____

_____

6. Describe how your thinking changed (if it changed) after you started to think realistically about the potential catastrophe. Does it seem more likely or less likely to happen?

_____

_____

_____

7. Do you think your fears about sleeping poorly are usually realistic? Why?

_____

_____

_____

8. Was it helpful to think through how you would handle the potential catastrophe?

Yes            No

# Wrapping Up

This book teaches teens thirty-one skills to help them relax and sleep well. Sleep science tells us that these skills work. But like any skill, they work only if you practice, and we hope you'll practice until you start to use them automatically. Just as in soccer or basketball, it's necessary to practice passing the ball over and over and over, so that when the time is right you can do it without even thinking and help your team score.

Once you're consistently sleeping well, you may think the hard work is behind you. However, for anyone who has ever struggled with insomnia, there's always a risk that it'll return. Sooner or later you're bound to go through a lot of stress, or you'll move to a new home and a new sleep environment, or you'll suffer jet lag from traveling across time zones. There's not much you can do to prevent life from rattling your sleep. Setbacks in the quality and quantity of your sleep will happen. That's okay, as long as you know how to come back from a setback and sleep well again.

We suggest you download the My Turning Setbacks into Comebacks Worksheet from http://www.newharbinger.com/41245. Having a plan will help you get your sleep back on track quickly using the skills that you've learned in this book.

We're sure that some of the skills in this book will work better for you than others. It's okay to have favorites. However, if at any point down the road you're having a hard time sleeping, and your favorite skills don't seem to be doing the job, look through the book again. You're likely to find one or two more skills that'll help you get some solid rest.

Although we've written this book for teens, the skills it teaches will also serve you when you're older. Every life change and every challenge, whether you're in college or in your first job, can disrupt your sleep. The good sleep strategies you've just learned will help you for many years to come.

Remember, your mind and body know how to sleep. They don't need your help. It's just a matter of you getting out of the way of this natural process so that your mind and body can get back to doing what they know how to do, and the skills you're practicing will make it easier.

Good luck and good sleep.

# Acknowledgments

We wish to thank Jonathan Barkin, Emily Berner, Joan Davidson, and Daniela Owen at the San Francisco Bay Area Center for Cognitive Therapy. They're superb clinician-scientists as well as thoughtful and caring colleagues. We appreciate their ongoing support of our professional development, including the writing of this workbook.

Monique would like to extend personal thanks to Dr. Allison Harvey and her team at the Golden Bear Sleep and Mood Research Clinic. Michael would like to extend personal thanks to Dr. Jacqueline B. Persons, who continues to support his professional development and to encourage projects like this workbook.

We wish to extend special thanks to Tesilya Hanauer, director of acquisitions at New Harbinger Publications. Her thoughtful feedback improved the overall quality of the manuscript and our confidence in the final product. We also thank the other members of the New Harbinger Publications team, who were unwaveringly patient and professional.

Every teen is different, but all are smart, resourceful, and amazing. With each teen we see in our practice, we learn something to help the next one. Thanks for passing it on.

We wish to thank our families for their support and encouragement of this project. We cannot imagine how we could have completed this workbook without you.

**Michael A. Tompkins, PhD, ABPP,** is a licensed psychologist who is board certified in behavioral and cognitive psychology. He is codirector of the San Francisco Bay Area Center for Cognitive Therapy; assistant clinical professor at the University of California, Berkeley; Diplomate and Founding Fellow of the Academy of Cognitive Therapy; and trainer and consultant for the Beck Institute for Cognitive Behavior Therapy. He is author or coauthor of numerous scholarly articles and chapters on cognitive behavioral therapy (CBT) and related topics, as well as seven books.

**Monique A. Thompson, PsyD,** is a licensed psychologist. She is a partner at the San Francisco Bay Area Center for Cognitive Therapy and a Diplomate of the Academy of Cognitive Therapy. She spent several years working as a research therapist at the Golden Bear Mood and Sleep Research Center at the University of California, Berkeley. She has published research on teen sleep treatments and memory interventions to improve CBT outcomes.

Foreword writer **Judith Beck, PhD,** is director of the Beck Institute for Cognitive Behavior Therapy, clinical associate professor of psychology in psychiatry at the University of Pennsylvania, and past president of the Academy of Cognitive Therapy. The daughter of influential founder of cognitive therapy, Aaron T. Beck, Beck resides in Bala Cynwyd, PA. She is author of *The Beck Diet Solution*.

# More ⏱ Instant Help Books for Teens

An Imprint of New Harbinger Publications

**THE STRESS REDUCTION
WORKBOOK FOR TEENS,
SECOND EDITION**

Mindfulness Skills to Help
You Deal with Stress

ISBN: 978-1684030187 / US $16.95

**THE ANXIETY WORKBOOK
FOR TEENS**

Activities to Help You Deal with
Anxiety & Worry

ISBN: 978-1572246034 / US $15.95

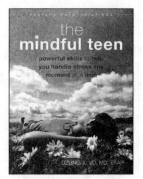

**THE MINDFUL TEEN**

Powerful Skills to Help You Handle
Stress One Moment at a Time

ISBN: 978-1626250802 / US $17.95

**THE WORRY WORKBOOK
FOR TEENS**

Effective CBT Strategies to Break the
Cycle of Chronic Worry & Anxiety

ISBN: 978-1626255845 / US $16.95

**THE PERFECTIONISM
WORKBOOK FOR TEENS**

Activities to Help You Reduce
Anxiety & Get Things Done

ISBN: 978-1626254541 / US $16.95

**THINK CONFIDENT,
BE CONFIDENT FOR TEENS**

A Cognitive Therapy Guide to
Overcoming Self-Doubt & Creating
Unshakable Self-Esteem

ISBN: 978-1608821136 / US $17.95

**newharbingerpublications**
1-800-748-6273 / newharbinger.com

(VISA, MC, AMEX / prices subject to change without notice)

Follow Us 🇫 🐦 📷 📌

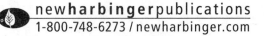

Don't miss out on new books in the subjects that interest you.
Sign up for our **Book Alerts** at **newharbinger.com/bookalerts** 🖱

Register your **new harbinger** titles for additional benefits!

When you register your **new harbinger** title—purchased in any format, from any source—you get access to benefits like the following:

- Downloadable accessories like printable worksheets and extra content

- Instructional videos and audio files

- Information about updates, corrections, and new editions

Not every title has accessories, but we're adding new material all the time.

Access free accessories in 3 easy steps:

**1.** Sign in at NewHarbinger.com (or **register** to create an account).

**2.** Click on **register a book**. Search for your title and click the **register** button when it appears.

**3.** Click on the **book cover or title** to go to its details page. Click on **accessories** to view and access files.

That's all there is to it!

If you need help, visit:

NewHarbinger.com/accessories

**new harbinger**
CELEBRATING
**40** YEARS

# a go-to guide for getting your zzzs

If you're like many teens, you probably aren't getting enough sleep. And is it any wonder? Between early school start times, mountains of homework, social media, friends, and late-night study sessions—there are plenty of distractions and disruptions that can get in the way of getting your Zzzs. So, how can you improve your sleep habits so you feel more alert and ready to face your day!

*The Insomnia Workbook for Teens* offers proven-effective tips and strategies to help you get to sleep and stay asleep. You'll learn about the different reasons you experience insomnia, tackle your own "sleep hazards" like caffeine and sugar, and discover skills for managing the stuff that keeps you awake at night so you can stop feeling drowsy and grumpy during the day. It's hard to reach your goals when you're feeling tired and run-down. This easy-to-use workbook will help you overcome insomnia and get the sleep you need to be your best.

> **"Finally, an evidence-based, easy-to-read, and sure-to-work guide for teens with sleep problems."**
> —KATHERINE MARTINEZ, PsyD, RPsych, psychologist and coauthor of *Your Anxious Mind*

**MICHAEL A. TOMPKINS, PhD, ABPP,** is a licensed psychologist and board certified in behavioral and cognitive psychology. He is codirector of the San Francisco Bay Area Center for Cognitive Therapy.

**MONIQUE A. THOMPSON, PsyD,** is a licensed psychologist. She is a partner at the San Francisco Bay Area Center for Cognitive Therapy and a Diplomate of the Academy of Cognitive Therapy.

**Instant Help Books**
An Imprint of New Harbinger Publications
www.newharbinger.com

Also available as an e-book

ISBN 978-1-68403-124-5

51795

9 781684 031245